46917

W9-BKE-521

46917

The Taste of Giverny

At Home with Monet and the American Impressionists

Editorial direction: Julie Rouart

Design and typesetting: Marine Gille

Color separation: Sele Offset, Turin

Translation: Josephine Bacon, American Pie, London

Copy-editing: Bernard Wooding

Originally published as *Giverny, un village impressionniste au temps de Monet*

© Flammarion, 2000

English-language edition © Flammarion Inc., 2000

Flammarion, 26 rue Racine, 75006 Paris, France

ISBN: 2-08013-687-9

Printed in Spain

The Taste of
Giverny

At Home with Monet and
the American Impressionists

Claire Joyes

Photography by
Jean-Marie del Moral
Styling by
Caroline Lebeau
Recipes by
Monique Mourgues

Flammarion

Contents

CHAPTER I

GIVERNY: A SIMPLE TALE

above

Louis Ritter,

Willows and Stream, c. 1887.

Oil on canvas.

Terra Foundation for the Arts

Collection, Chicago.

left

The Epte. This tributary of the

Seine, that flows past Giverny,

was popular with painters.

The local women and children

swam in it during the summer.

It can be stated with certainty that all, or nearly all, villages are old, but some are undoubtedly much older than others. The village of Giverny was born about four thousand years ago, which makes it very young compared with the Earth itself, but a reasonable age for any place destined to become of historical interest. And like a person who has lived to a ripe old age, it has witnessed a number of events, ranging through the commonplace, scandalous, edifying, and occasionally horrifying.

Strange as it may seem, villages have no idea of what may be in store for them. They are unprepared, unaware that it takes little to suddenly thrust them into history. It may be a single incident, a tragedy, an alliance, a site or the presence, however discreet, of a celebrity who has chosen the place as a retreat from the world.

A thousand things could have wrenched this little town, which had no particular vocation, from its peaceful anonymity and precipitated it willy-nilly into the horrors or delights—depending on your viewpoint—of fame. Giverny, like other villages unconcerned about renown, led an existence that, although not tranquil (due to the upheavals of the millennia—general instability, incessant wars and invasions, a few plagues), was at least inconspicuous.

Babylon owes its fame to its hanging gardens, Troy to the trick played on it with the extraordinary horse, and Alexandria to its great library that went up in flames. Even Perpignan in southern France was rendered famous by Salvador Dalí, who proclaimed its railroad station the center of the universe. We tend

above

Guy Rose,

Giverny Hillside, 1890–1895.

Oil on canvas.

Terra Foundation for the Arts

Collection, Chicago.

GIVERNY: A SIMPLE TALE

to remember that which touches upon the surreal, the magical aspect of things. What will be read about Giverny several centuries hence in encyclopedias, or whatever takes their place?

Giverny lies inland, although it is close to Vernon, formerly an important trading port. It overlooks the Seine, a powerful river which irrigates and floods, and was for centuries the main transport route. The Seine is joined at this point by the Epte, which cuts between two densely wooded, flared banks. These are overlooked in the north by wild hills, rich with game, that are often covered in mist, although in the fifteenth century the southern slopes were planted with vines, which do not thrive in foggy sites. At some point, the land beside the rivers was deforested to gain access to the rich alluvial soils washed by the movements and caprices of the Seine.

This is a landscape of long valleys. The land is open and unfenced, and there are no walls protecting the villages. Houses, each surrounded by a wall pierced by a single gate, are clustered into hamlets and each hamlet is dominated by a handsome, Romanesque church completed by a Gothic transept and dedicated to Sainte Radegonde or Saint Roch. Little is known of Giverny's past, since the memory of a village is like a huge unexplored loft—sometimes it is packed with abandoned memorabilia eagerly awaiting chance discovery by archivists driven by the eternal fear of failing to transmit, and sometimes it is a vast, empty wasteland consigned to oblivion. We know that its Latin name was Warnacum and that from an early period there was a family by the name of Giverny, but all trace of it disappeared in the eighteenth century. Like the rest of this part of Europe, Giverny had a few Gallic forebears before coming under Roman rule. The Romans were followed successively by the Merovingians and the Carolingians. In the late eighth century, the inhabitants of the village would have witnessed King Charles the Bald, who came

above

THEODORE EARL BUTLER,

Apple Trees in Blossom.

Oil on canvas. Private collection.

double page following

The Epte, lined with tall trees

reflected in the water, marks the

boundary of Normandy.

above

The Romanesque church at Giverny and its cemetery.

left

THEODORE ROBINSON,

From the Hill, c. 1889. Oil on canvas.

Terra Foundation for the Arts Collection, Chicago.

CHAPTER I
GIVERNY: A SIMPLE TALE

to parlay with the Barbarians camped by the mouth of the Epte. While it is true that this same Charles the Bald mentioned Giverny in the list of properties owned by the Abbey of Saint Denis in Vexin, no chronicle has been handed down relating the importance of the village or indicating that it was the scene of one of those fights to the death whose true aim was to share the spoils left behind by the departing Roman occupation. A few years after glimpsing Charles the Bald, the villagers must have watched in terror as the Viking armada sailed upriver, having burnt and pillaged the abbeys at the mouth of the Seine, on their way to the Ile d'Oscelle, a few miles further on.

The village contains no plaque recording the presence of such early rulers as the Nordic Osbern d'Esquetot or his successor, Charles François Toustain, lord of Fontebosc, Limésy, and Giverny, and king's musketeer. Also absent are the names of Brèvedent and Le Lorier, who were prominent in founding "modern" Giverny, although one of their descendants was mayor after the French Revolution. On the other hand, a certain Messire Jean Coulbeaux, about whom nothing is known at all, has a delightful little passageway named for him.

The medieval period left the deepest impression on Giverny's appearance, still visible in the largest houses, the outlying districts, and the street names. The village was a dependency of the barony of Gasny and one of the numerous agricultural holdings of the wealthy Abbey of Saint-Ouen, famous for its copying workshop. The monks, whose skills at building could have led them

above right

The church and cemetery at Giverny
in the early nineteenth century.

facing page

The Seine near Giverny

as it looks today.

GIVERNY. - Les Prairies

Phot. A. L., Vernon

top

LILLA CABOT PERRY,

Autumn Afternoon, Giverny. Oil on Canvas.

Terra Foundation for the Arts Collection, Chicago.

bottom

The meadows at Giverny.

Postcard, Toulgouat Collection, Giverny.

to write one of those great pages in the history of architecture for which they frequently showed such genius, chose instead to produce solid edifices whose purpose was well defined. These included the Ferme de la Dîme with its large tithe barn, the farm later called the Ferme de la Côte, the house called the Maison Bleue, the Moutier (monastery), and the Chennevières mill. A network of underground passages (which exist today and are still being discovered during modern building work) linked the houses and made it possible to reach the hills and flee from invaders.

The monks' most valuable legacy was the ingenious and delightful Ru canal, which was full of fish and eels, attracted large numbers of waterfowl and, most importantly, supplied fresh water to the abbey fishpond. The latter was fenced in and carefully guarded against poachers. The Ru became an artificial tributary of the Epte, which in places ran too far from the village farmland to be useful for irrigation. The monks installed a system of sluice gates with which they could flood and irrigate the surrounding meadows; these are still in working order today. The Ru ran closer to the village than the Epte, beside the ancient Chemin du Roy (as would the railroad later on), although its course was slightly altered by Monet when he built his famous water-lily pond.

For centuries, the village thus lived to the timeless rhythm of agricultural labor and various rites secular and religious. Paradoxically, it was the monks who initiated the first event which overthrew the established order, at the beginning of the seventeenth century, when the Abbey of Saint-Ouen sold its Giverny

above

A street in Giverny that runs beside the Romanesque church and its cemetery. On winter mornings, the streets of Giverny are wrapped in mist.

right

DAWSON DAWSON-WATSON,

Giverny: Road Looking West toward Church, c. 1890.

Oil on Canvas.

Terra Foundation for the Arts Collection, Chicago.

following double page

The mill at Fourgues, ten miles from
Giverny. Monet's friend Coquand
owned a beautiful château in Fourgues.

left

The old Chennevières mill.

Its owner, Stanton Young, used

to call it the "Petit Moulin."

Postcard, Toulgouat Collection.

above

Fall in Giverny.

Most of the houses in Giverny are

covered in Virginia creeper and

the gardens are luxuriant.

property, a move which providentially saved the district from the worst excesses of the French Revolution.

As always, especially in those distant times when the sacred and the profane intermingled, the church and its adjoining cemetery traditionally had the privilege of granting sanctuary. Even though the little concourse in front of the church was occasionally used for worship, a shameless peasant would occasionally graze his cattle there. It was here that the court of law sat and the notary engrossed his legal documents in this open-air office. All of this would take place just across from a leaning standing stone once called "the stone of the sick." Some maintained that it was reputed to cure scurvy, but it is more likely to have been used as a remedy against the Black Death, as it was within the "sphere of influence" of Saint Roch.

Things remained relatively quiet up until 1861, the year the Compagnie des Chemins de Fer de l'Ouest laid a single-track railroad through the area known as "Le Grand Pré," thus enabling "the little train" to chug up and down for nearly a hundred years. The train helped transform the landscape, paving the way for the spread of an unfortunate architectural Esperanto. Twenty-two years later Monet chose to live in Giverny, and two or three years after his arrival, facilitated by the rail link with Paris, the peaceful American invasion began. The village was thus brutally shaken out of its torpor, although it took at least ten years for it to become an important American artists' colony in Europe, numerically at least, and a fashionable place to visit. It is extraordinary to think that the landscape which enchanted all these artists in the last quarter of the nineteenth century had remained almost unchanged since the Middle Ages.

top

Giverny seen from the Hôtel Baudy at the beginning of the
twentieth century. The haystacks, a popular subject for painters,
could even be seen in the heart of the village.

bottom

The railroad was built in 1861 by the Compagnie des Chemins de
Fer de l'Ouest and linked Giverny with Vernon. The presence of
the train was not unconnected with Monet's arrival twenty years
later. In the background can be seen the church and the hills.
Postcard, Toulgouat Collection, Giverny.

following double page

John Leslie Breck,
Morning Fog and Sun, 1892. Oil on canvas.
Terra Foundation for the Arts Collection, Chicago.

Paris, the Seine, its old bistros and the Louvre were popular haunts of artists who had crossed the Atlantic to study art in the city's studios, reputed to be the finest in the world. Without Paris, Giverny would have had an entirely different destiny.

A CERTAIN NEED FOR EUROPE

above

Detail of a mosaic in one of the arcades at the Palais Royal in Paris.

facing page

The Café Allard has retained the charm of the old Parisian bistros from the end of the nineteenth century.

I t is impossible to move abruptly from one era to another and remain unchanged. Giverny's adventure—for it was, indeed, an adventure—swept it from the serenity of a traditional way of life, with its regular seasonal rituals, to an era of noise and bustle, punctuated by the incessant comings and goings of people who had arrived from elsewhere but were to be found everywhere— in the streets, on the hills, in the meadows, and even on the water. The various causes of this metamorphosis were Paris, the "little train," Claude Monet, the Hôtel Baudy, and, above all, the lure of an idyllic existence in the countryside, bathed in the special light of the Seine Valley.

For the local peasants who, like their ancestors before them, toiled day in day out to tame nature (with varying degrees of success), and who were totally at the mercy of its whims, this new phenomenon was incomprehensible. They had got used to the presence of the self-absorbed and laconic Monet, but this invasion of strangers lodging at the inn, looking for houses to rent, would doubtless have left them nonplussed. What on earth were they doing here? Most of them could hardly speak any French and some spoke none at all! The villagers, cautious and reserved by nature, were suddenly thrust into the adventure of having to express themselves in simple language, abandoning their *patois*-laden French in favor of New World English. The strangers for their part were forced to try and understand the local archaic French. What would they have done without eloquent gestures and pocket dictionaries?

The presence of Monet and his family alone as permanent residents would have changed little or nothing in village life, but the successive waves of artists flooding the district from 1885 through to the outbreak of World War I—a form of cultural tourism par excellence—brought about more changes in a single decade than had occurred in all the preceding centuries, which had so closely resembled one another that it was hard to tell what was past and what was future. Fortunately, this eventful period became one of expansion and openness, in which new attitudes emerged, together with widespread prosperity. The artists eventually populated Giverny as they had settled in places such as Grez, Barbizon, Concarneau, and Pont-Aven.

One thing is certain, the reputation of Giverny and its artists' colony, the phenomenon of Monet and the American painters, could never have happened without Paris. Giverny, like all the artists' colonies in the provinces, was but a satellite of the Parisian academies of art, and in particular the École Nationale des Beaux-Arts (clearly, artists were not discouraged by the composer, Éric Satie, who remarked, "The air in Paris is so bad that I always boil it before breathing it").

In the nineteenth century, the "grand tour" of Europe was regarded as a key element in the education of both aspiring American artists and the children of wealthy American families, just as refined Europeans at the time regarded knowledge of Rome, Greece, and Egypt as a fundamental prerequisite for a rounded education. The same values prevailed on either side of the Atlantic.

If the truth be told, there was a lot of confusion in European minds as to the true reasons for this American need for Europe. It was not just the peasants of Brie, Picardy, Brittany, and Normandy who were surprised by the attraction of Paris and the French countryside. The American continent has large tracts

above

Inscription on the Pont des Arts, which links the Louvre to the Académie des Beaux-Arts. Paris, the artistic capital of the world at the end of the nineteenth century, honors its sculpture gardens, which served as subjects for the many artists who came to study in the city.

facing page

The Musée du Louvre attracted
many painters who came to copy
the Old Masters in order to
improve their technique.

following double page

Sculpture in the
Tuileries Gardens, Paris.

above

Studios at the Académie Julian in Paris in the late nineenth century.

In the French academies, nudes were painted from life, an exercise

that was not possible in the art schools of the United States.

of every kind of forest, yet Professor George Loring Brown, who studied in Rome and became a student of Isabey, declared that the forest of Barbizon ought to be transported to Beacon Hill in Boston. Was he being serious? His remark was echoed by Salvador Dalí, who solemnly declared to Julien Green (who had been living in Giverny for several seasons with his sister Anne): "There are no landscapes in America, there are only 'geo-lo-gi-cal accidents.'"

The Americans did have landscapes, of course, as well as farmers and country scenes, and they had them long before 1851, when Cyrus Hall McCormick exhibited a picture at the Great Exhibition in London showing reaping machines. They even had haystacks, such as those painted by Martin Johnson Heade in the boggy landscape at Newburyport (1865–70) or those depicted by Dawson Dawson-Watson (who was a guest at the Hôtel Baudy for a few seasons), in Connecticut in 1895, after his stay in France.

Not only did the Americans have beautiful landscapes, but there were also plenty of art schools, especially in the big cities such as New York, Boston, Philadelphia, Washington, and Chicago. The painters who spent time at Giverny, such as Robinson, Butler, Metcalf, Hale, Perry, Rose, Frieseke, and Graecen, were no mere amateurs. They had graduated from the National Academy of Design, the Art Students League, the Cowles Art School, the Pennsylvania Academy, the Corcoran Art School, and the Massachusetts Normal School, as well as the Chicago Academy of Design, which was to become the prestigious Art Institute of Chicago. All of them had spent time in these institutions before studying in Paris at the Académie Julian, the Académie Colarossi, the Académie de la Grande-Chaumière, or the famous studio run by Carolus-Duran at Montparnasse. The most courageous of them attended the École des Beaux-Arts, the perfect addition to the résumé of an accomplished American artist.

top

Corridor at the École des Beaux-Arts in Paris, one of the most prestigious art schools of the period.

bottom

Picture on display in a gallery in the Nouvelle Athènes neighborhood in Paris.

facing page

Mas, the famous nineteenth-century dealer of engravings, is still in business today.

The presbytery in Giverny with
its half-timbering. The stone
steps lead to the tombs of Claude
Monet and his family.

top

The little train at Giverny. The single-track line ran alongside
the Epte and linked Giverny with Vernon, enabling
the American artists to join the master of Impressionism.
Postcard, Toulgouat Collection, Giverny.

bottom

William Howard Hart (Peggy Hart), James Butler (Jimi),
Marthe Butler, Theodore Earl Butler, Alice Monet, and Lily Butler
at Vernon station, about to leave for a stay on the Normandy coast.
Photograph, Toulgouat Collection, Giverny.

facing page

Monet's first studio, which
was later turned into a
drawing room. Monet kept
paintings he didn't want to
sell there.

top

Claude Monet at his desk in
his first studio. Photograph by
Thérèse Bonney. Toulgouat
Collection, Giverny.

bottom

Palette and tubes of paint.

Ironically, many of these painters who flocked to Paris were from families which had just disembarked from the emigrant ships anchored off Manhattan Island. These budding artists were determined to attack the landscapes and academies of France. Nothing deterred them, certainly not the heroically endured discomfort and appallingly dangerous conditions of the crossing, which for some was an odyssey. They arrived initially in schooners, then in large steamships. Some even made it in banana boats passing through the Straits of Gibraltar. The standard sea route was from New York to Liverpool or Southampton in England, from where one could take a ferry to France or Germany.

A study cited by Barbara Weiberg is revealing: no fewer than 2,200 American artists born about 1880 studied in Paris, one third of whom were women. In the 1890s, the Mormons even sent a delegation of artists from their community to Paris, where their tasks included learning how to paint frescoes so that they could decorate the Mormon religious buildings on their return. In the first half of the nineteenth century, there was growing recognition in the United States of a need for better teaching together with public galleries where good art could be seen. A combination of convention, conformity, and religious tradition led the artists to opt initially for London, then Munich, Düsseldorf, Florence and Rome. In the second half of the century, Paris became the artistic capital of Europe and the École des Beaux-Arts was universally deemed to provide the best teaching at the time. In order to reach a high level of achievement in painting, sculpture, and architecture, it was therefore necessary to visit Paris (although the city's popularity may also have been partly due to its image in the American psyche as an unconventional city populated by libertines). In those days, the influence of France was even felt on the other side of the world, in

San Francisco, where lectures on anatomy by Léon Bonnat were being read out to students at the California School of Design.

The forerunner of the École des Beaux-Arts was the Académie Royale de Peinture et de Sculpture, founded by Louis XIV in 1648. Artists from all over the world benefited from this establishment, especially the less affluent, since the teaching was free and open to students of all nationalities. However, students had to pass a tough entrance examination covering various disciplines, including "general culture." A further requirement was that you had to be male: it was not until 1897 that both sexes were admitted.

It is not possible to detail here all the events, political and artistic, that marked this turbulent period, which witnessed not only the fall of the Second Empire of Napoleon III but also a certain scandalous art exhibition held on the premises of the photographer Nadar on the Boulevard des Capucines in 1874, which resulted in the coining of the term "Impressionism." Suffice it to say, there was plenty to cause unrest in the academies of art and to provide controversial topics of conversation for many decades to come.

Most of the aspiring American painters were inspired by the lesser, but fashionable, talents of Bastien Lepage, Puvis de Chavannes, Couture, Gérôme, Bouguereau, and Cabanel. In Monet's circle at Giverny, however, the artists were faced with a momentous and difficult dilemma: should they become Impressionists or not?

above

Monet's water-lily pond as it looks today. During the creation of the pond, the Ru canal was diverted slightly to supply it with water.

following double page

JOHN LESLIE BRECK,
The Epte at Giverny, c. 1887.
Oil on canvas. Terra Foundation
for the Arts Collection, Chicago.

above

Claude Monet's house, which has now been turned into a museum.

This former farmhouse was modified on several occasions by

Monet, who had two studios built.

right

Claude Monet (in the foreground) with his friend,

the painter William H. Hart. Monet is carrying furs, brought back

from his voyage to Norway, which he used to keep himself warm

when out in his automobile.

A Certain Need for Europe

facing page

The "open air studio" on the
banks of the Epte. Impoverished
painters propped their canvases
against the branches of trees
as makeshift easels.

left

Dawson Dawson-Watson,

Beet Field, 1891. Oil on canvas.

Private collection.

following double page

Monet's water-lily pond.

above

View of Giverny in the fall.
Postcard, Toulgouat Collection,
Giverny.

facing page

Madame Baudy's grocery store
stocked all the ingredients
required for making an Anglo-
American breakfast—porridge,
cornflakes, maple syrup, and tea
imported from England.

CHAPTER III
DAILY LIFE IN GIVERNY

top

CAROLUS-DURAN, *Portrait of
Claude Monet*, 1867. Oil on canvas.
Musée Marmottan-Monet, Paris.

bottom

The Butler children returning from
their first communion with "Bonne,"
their grandmother (Alice Monet), May
1905. Toulgouat Collection, Giverny.

The end of Giverny's tranquil existence was already on the
cards prior to Monet's arrival in 1883, and even before
Metcalf and Robinson visited the village during a walking tour
a couple of years after the Master's arrival. The year is 1867, a
year loaded with signs and portents: Carolus-Duran painted
Monet's portrait and dedicated it to him in friendship; the Salon
jury rejected the latter's painting *Women in the Garden*, for which
Camille, his first wife, had been one of the models; the Universal Exposition proved one of the most significant for Western
artists, among them several from the Giverny colony; and Japan
reappeared on the world scene.

As always, important events combine with apparently
insignificant incidents with unexpected repercussions. At the
Universal Exposition, the businessman Ernest Hoschedé built a
pavilion. Hoschedé was the father of Suzanne, the *Woman with
a Parasol* and the future Mrs. Theodore Butler. He was also a
collector and patron of the arts, including the Impressionists. He
bought Monet's paintings from an early stage and for a large
amount of money. These included such works as *Impression,
Sunrise, St. Germain l'Auxerrois,* the first "London" series, and
paintings of St. Lazare railroad station.

In 1876, Claude Monet was commissioned by Ernest
Hoschedé to decorate the round drawing room (Salon en
Rotonde) at the Château de Rottembourg at Montgeron, the
estate to the south of Paris given to his wife Alice by her father.
No one, including Alice, had any inkling at that time that

Le Moutier, known at the time as
"the Monastery," whose barn was
converted into a sculpture studio
for Frederick MacMonnies.
Photograph by Pierre Toulgouat.

Hoschedé would fall into financial ruin only two years later,
forcing him to sell his collection (two of the decorations in the
round drawing room would soon find their way into Russian
collections). Alice was in turn forced to sell the château and
began to live a simple village life, taking in the young American artists as boarders.

The bankruptcy brought Alice closer to Monet, with whom
she had struck up a friendship when he was working at Rottembourg. In 1878, the Hoschedés moved to Vétheuil, near
Argenteuil (only a few miles from Giverny), where they lived
side by side with Monet and Camille. Shortly after the death of
Camille in 1879, the relationship between Alice and Monet
became "official," and the couple moved together, along with
Alice's six children, first to Poissy, and then on to Giverny in 1883.

We are jumping ahead, however; to fit our Giverny puzzle
together, we should return to Monet's portraitist, Carolus-Duran.
"My dear Carolus," as Monet used to call him, taught painting
in Paris. His social connections and artistic talents attracted a
number of students, including a strong contigent of Americans,
who referred to his studio on the Boulevard Montparnasse as
the "81." The "81" opened in 1873 with twelve students, including Will Low, Caroll Beckwith, and Robert Allan Mowbray
Stevenson, who was a second cousin to the writer Robert Louis
Stevenson. The following year, Dr. Sargent, only too happy to
curtail his cosmopolitan wanderings, arrived to introduce his
son, John Singer Sargent, to the studio. It was Beckwith who
opened the door, as Carolus-Duran was busy correcting his students' work. Beckwith and Sargent were friends of Paul Helleu,
who was himself a friend of Monet and Carolus. Sargent and
Monet became close friends from 1876 onward. Soon Kenyon
Cox, then Theodore Robinson, both of them future residents of
Giverny, spent some time at the "81," as did Sargent's friend

above

The Maison Rose, at the time the
Pension Revert. Philip and Lilian
Hale, then Peggy Hart
and his wife, and much later,
Isadora Duncan, all stayed here.
Photograph by Pierre Toulgouat.

Claude Monet (on the right)

with his son-in-law Theodore

Earl Butler, waiting for Sylvain

the chauffeur. Despite his passion

for automobiles, Monet never

drove a car in his life.

Toulgouat Collection, Giverny.

CHAPTER III
DAILY LIFE IN GIVERNY

CHAPTER III
DAILY LIFE IN GIVERNY

facing page

Reconstruction of the entrance

hall in a house near Giverny,

similar to those lived in by

American artists and their

families.

Theodore Butler, who for a while lived in the same building as Carolus-Duran. All these people spent time at Giverny and, apart from Will Low and Stevenson for some reason, they were all in Monet's circle of friends.

Monet and Carolus were not the only magnets attracting artists to Giverny. After "my dear Carolus," there came "my dear Coquand" and "my dear Deconchy." The painter Paul Coquand, who had studied in Marseilles and Paris, decided to move to the country because of his wife's delicate health. He took over his father's château at Fourges near the river Epte, a few miles from Giverny. Coquand knew Monet, but was also the catalyst for a visit in 1885 from his friend and former fellow student at the Academy, Willard Metcalf. Metcalf had a genuine love of nature and was a keen ornithologist. He went hiking in the countryside, which was in full bloom at that time of year, and he would often return to Giverny to paint. During another visit, he had a less gratifying experience when he enquired at the inn about accommodation for the night and had the door slammed in his face…

Ferdinand Deconchy, another painter who was friendly with Monet, owned a country house at Gasny, which was even closer than Coquand's estate. It was Deconchy who introduced Monet to the important collector Raymond Koechlin, as well as to Theodore Robinson.

In the country, whether people visit with each other or ignore one another, word gets around, and everyone knows who everyone is. This was especially true in the days when villages were still mainly inhabited by peasants and any prominent new arrival would soon be noticed. But where the "outsiders" quickly established their social networks, how the locals would react to this increasingly large number of foreigners in their village was another matter.

above

American artists relaxing

in the Hôtel Baudy.

Photograph, formerly in Madame

Baudy's collection.

The local residents had little idea of what some of the painters had had to endure in order to be able to come and work in their village. Quite apart from the perilous crossing of the Atlantic, some of the Americans were penniless and had worked incredibly hard in order to be able to come and paint in Europe. They mostly came to study and had little time to waste, which may go some way to explain their apparent lack of curiosity concerning the host country. Here in France, one had to work hard to stand a chance of simply exhibiting at the Salon, let alone winning a medal. Perhaps if the *cultivants*, as the local farmers were called in Giverny, had realized all this, they might have been less dismissive of the newcomers than they were—at first.

The new arrivals intrigued the locals, who were suspicious by nature (many had never journeyed as far as the next village). For a long time, whenever one of these newcomers approached, villagers would turn and scrutinize the stranger. Yet with the passage of time, the peasants heading for their fields in the early morning got used to seeing Monet, a thick sweater thrown over his shoulders, going out to paint, or Blanche pushing the wheelbarrow containing the artist's materials (when she wasn't painting alongside her American friends, notably John L. Breck and Theodore Butler). Butler had devised an unusual piece of equipment, a mobile studio-caravan with windows, sliding doors, and shafts so that it could be pulled. What was most unusual about it, though, was that Butler himself was the horse! But by now, the village was full of so many new faces that no one was much surprised by anything.

above

Reconstruction of a room in which the fabrics are inspired by Japanese prints.

top left

Still life featuring the oriental vases which were very fashionable at the period.

right

Theodore Earl Butler,

Penitence. Pastel.

Toulgouat Collection, Giverny.

above

THEODORE EARL BUTLER,

Untitled. Pastel.

Toulgouat Collection, Giverny.

facing page

FREDERICK CARL FRIESEKE,

Unraveling Silk, 1915 (detail). Oil on canvas.

Terra Foundation for the Arts Collection,

Chicago.

Among the new arrivals were families like the Johnstons, who had discovered Giverny while on a boat trip and got into the habit of crossing the Atlantic every year to spend the summer there. Whether they came from Boston, Philadelphia, New York, or elsewhere, whether they lodged at the inn or in private homes, all of them eventually integrated quite successfully into the village. Artists and villagers lived cheek-by-jowl and frequently surprised each other; they would meet in the countryside, in church, and in the various cafés. In the summer, tennis matches were held, while in the winter ice fairs illuminated by paper lanterns were organized.

As for Monet, he greeted the first arrivals with pleasure. He always refused to teach in the strictest sense of the word, but he was happy to talk about painting and offer advice to Breck, Butler, Deconchy, to Blanche Hoschedé during their life together, or to Lilla Cabot Perry, who was his next-door neighbor for four summers. Robinson notes in his journal for August 15, 1892: "I have had a call from the Master. His favorite painting of mine is *View of Vernon*. It is the closest to my ideal. He told me it was the best landscape I have painted."

Monet soon found that he was consulted too frequently for comfort and was obliged to shut his door. After all, he had come to Giverny for peace and quiet and was now faced with a disruptive invasion. He began to see only those people who had been referred to him by friends and seriously considered leaving the area. This was a time when he was painting the *Haystacks* series right outside his front door, so he needed plenty of peace and time for meditation. Yet people kept coming to admire his work! It is not that Monet lacked imagination, but there is nothing worse than seeing one's subjects and ideas filched and copied. "To run away to a village and make it the center of the world," in the

right

THEODORE EARL BUTLER,

An Evening with the Butler Family

(detail). Oil on canvas.

Portrayed are Guy and Ethel

Rose, Edmund Greacen and his

wife, Marthe Butler in the

foreground and Lili and Jimi

Butler in the background.

Toulgouat Collection, Giverny.

words of Jules Renard, was the very last thing he wanted. He did continue to receive visits, however, but simply became more selective of his company.

Meanwhile, the Hoschedé-Monet children, wearing cloche hats in pastel colors, would chat to Michel Monet and his brother Jean-Pierre as they worked, covered in engine oil and axle grease, on their invention of a mysterious vehicle. On other occasions, they would run over the hills with Metcalf or the local priest, collecting wild plants. There were so many people: insect collectors with their butterfly nets and collecting boxes, fishermen and hunters, accompanied by Mr. and Mrs. Rose, the Salerous and the Butlers, picnickers, saucy artist's models from Paris, and painters, many of whom were women (Will Low, during a brief stay at the Baudy, observed that most of the guests were female). Then, as soon as the sun came out in July, everyone escaped to the coast to swim in the sea and find new subjects to paint.

Before long, at any time of day, the messenger boy from the Baudy could be encountered on his way to deliver the large picnic hampers and other baskets of food prepared by the inn. Gaston's horse-drawn station wagon would be on its way to or from the Baudy, with its complement of elegant travelers. No one noticed Cézanne's arrival; nor were they particularly surprised at the advent of the "Casse-Museau," Caillebotte's handsome floating studio, nor to see Pissarro, who often came by train. Not even John Singer Sargent, Radimsky, Octave Mirbeau, or even Lilla Cabot Perry on her bicycle caused a stir. If the truth be told, even though they had an inkling that, as they put it, "these are all swells," with the exception of the leading French politician, Georges Clemenceau, it would be many years before those destined to rise to fame among the visitors would do so.

Even at the tiny post office, the size of a telephone kiosk, the postmistress was not impressed by the names she encountered,

above

Monet's home. James (or Jimi) Butler sitting on the sofa in the library, also known as the mauve drawing room. The famous prints by Hokusai, *The Wave* and *Mount Fuji*, can be seen on the wall. Toulgouat Collection, Giverny.

facing page

Tea at Monet's home in the mauve drawing room (the library) included scones and muffins with home-made jam.

facing page

THEODORE EARL BUTLER,

Lili Butler Reading at the Butler House, 1908.

Oil on canvas. Terra Foundation for the Arts

Collection, Chicago.

top

THEODORE EARL BUTLER,

The Artist's Children, James and Lili, 1896.

Oil on canvas. Terra Foundation for the Arts

Collection, Chicago.

bottom

THEODORE EARL BUTLER,

Untitled. Pastel.

Toulgouat Collection, Giverny.

while Giverny station did a brisk trade in despatching bulging crates of paintings to dealers in Paris and throughout the world. Soon, famous names in the art world such as Georges Petit, Boussod, Valadon, Durand-Ruel, and later Bernheim were as familiar to the station porter as were those of the museums.

The influx of artists roused Giverny as if from a long sleep. Time had stood still for so long but now it moved at a great pace. The world was changing fast, but in the village no one realized that a point of no return had been reached, that this was more than just the introduction of a few crazy ideas by a few vacationers that would blow over after a few seasons. The place was a hive of activity. Painters painted, spoiled for choice of subject-matter, the peasants tilled the soil, but also rented out their houses and sold their barns whose tiled roofs were now broken up by the insertion of large panes of glass.

The austerity of peasant life contrasted sharply with the agitation engendered by this large colony of artists. Nevertheless, most people seemed to adapt well to the new situation and even to derive some benefit from it, however modest. The local farmer's wives were good-hearted souls, and sometimes took pity on these painters and their paraphernalia, giving them a lift in their horse-drawn wagons, or on occasion towing poor Robinson who was hauling equipment that was much too heavy for him as he struggled to get to the Grosse Pierre to work on his *Views*.

Robinson notes in his journal for June 5, 1892: "I was interrupted while hard at work on my *View of Vernon No. 2* by a thunderstorm followed by a heavy shower. Old Mr. Gaillard told me that he was delighted with it, for his flowers and his garden. He had worked in a telegraph office for thirty years and now appreciated the opportunity of being able to work outdoors: 'I'm happy as a god.'"

CHAPTER III
DAILY LIFE IN GIVERNY

right and facing page

When not outside painting, many of the artists wrote letters and journals. Watson even produced *Le courrier innocent,* a satirical journal published in the village and illustrated by his painter friends.

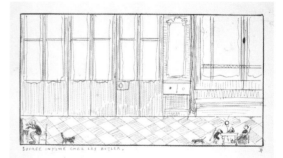

above

"At Home at the Butlers," invitation card designed by Theodore Earl Butler. Toulgouat Collection, Giverny.

It is true that Giverny's land and climate was kind to locals and visitors alike. Nature in this part of the world was abundant, well cared for, and celebrated. In the village, farm entrances were flanked by walnut trees, the boundaries of properties were marked out with rows of ash trees, the narrow streets were hedged with hawthorn and hornbeam, and in the orchards, the apple trees acting as wind-breaks were carefully tended. The meadows were lush, willows lined the riverbanks, and poplars abounded, contributing to the special quality of light. There were vast fields of grain—wheat, barley, and hemp, the latter still being spun and woven by groups of local women. The sight of the fruit trees in blossom halfway up the hill was delightful in spring, and the wild irises in the marshes delighted the botanists. The painters contrasted this display with that of the Rue des Grands-Jardins, where, since time immemorial, allotments had been cultivated by the Ru canal to make them easy to water. These geometrically aligned plots looked like a huge checkerboard.

One wonders how the farm worker plowing his field on the Plain of Ajoux must have reacted when the haystacks he had just built or the poplar trees he had planted, all part of his everyday labors, were lovingly reproduced on canvas by these strangers from a distant land.

And what about the odd clothing worn by these artists, with their velvet baggy pants? Did they buy wooden clogs to add a little "local color"? No one is sure. Some of the artists went boating and canoeing, the women wore cycling bloomers, and some donned swimming costumes with suspenders in order to bathe in the Seine, the Epte, and the Ru. Monet's studio-boat was moored at the island known as the Ile aux Orties (Stinging Nettle Island), and its roof was used as a diving-board by the children, who were often joined by André and Jeanne Sisley.

top

The artists take a well-earned rest on a hill during an excursion.

Photograph, Toulgouat Collection, Giverny.

bottom

The painter John Leslie Breck (sitting) with Blanche Hoschedé, Alice, Maine and

Suzanne Hoschedé, Claude Monet, Blair Bruce, and Henry Fitch Taylor in Monet's garden.

Photograph, Toulgouat Collection, Giverny.

below

EDMUND CHARLES TARBELL,

In the Orchard, 1891.

Oil on canvas. Terra Foundation

for the Arts Collection, Chicago.

CHAPTER III
DAILY LIFE IN GIVERNY

below

Theodore Earl Butler,

Garden Path Leading to the Gate.

Oil on canvas.

Toulgouat Collection, Giverny.

above

Path in Monet's garden.

Life in the village had a certain simplicity. At daybreak, the blacksmith's hammer resounded on the anvil like banging on the gates of hell. After all, the handsome Percheron cart-horses, the pride of farms from the Epte Valley to the Plateau des Bruyères, had to be kept well shod. They were harnessed to wagons in arrow-formations of five horses, encouraged by their drovers using those monotonous sounds that have remained unchanged since time immemorial. For the festival of Rogation Sunday, the fly-swatter manes and the long tails of these handsome beasts would be braided. Then there was the grinding of the wheels of the carts pushed by the laundrywomen as they made their way to the public wash-houses, gossiping as they went, reveling in the good fortune of having so much to talk about in those exciting times. Rain fell heavily into the round water butts of the farmyards which were used for irrigation. Other familiar sounds would have included the distant hoots of tugboats on the Seine and the puffing of the little train completing one of its four daily journeys.

The little train ran so regularly you could set your watch by it, and you could get it to stop for you right out in the middle of the countryside to load a row-boat on board, so you could avoid having to pass through several locks, thereby reaching the location chosen for painting more quickly. White sunshades were dotted over the landscape, under which artists were painting young girls from the village. Although these models were less expensive than those in Paris, they had to be chaperoned by their mothers, who would sit at a distance embroidering. It is not certain that it was the case in Giverny, but in other artists' colonies, the chaperone also had to be paid!

The artists worked hard and they visited each other's studios to admire their work. On July 24, 1892, Robinson, who had never been a great feminist, wrote: "Cloudy morning, which is

left

Claude Monet and his son Michel

taking photographs near the

lily pond. Toulgouat Collection,

Giverny.

following double page

FREDERICK CARL FRIESEKE,

Tea Time in a Giverny Garden.

Oil on canvas. Terra Foundation

for the Arts Collection, Chicago.

no good for me. After breakfast, a lot of women came and enthused over my paintings, as is usually the case. I think they are bored." Among themselves, they were not always charitable, hence the allusion, from an unknown source, to Thomas Harrison's "daubs."

Other painters, such as Frieseke, Leftwich Dodge, Mac-Monnies, and Ritman, disappeared behind the high walls of gardens in order to paint nudes. These high-walled kitchen gardens were not unusual at the time, though few of them were available for painting naked models! The drystone walls around the houses had been built to protect the farms from marauders, to shelter them from the wind, or merely to prevent wandering chickens or other animals from escaping. Unfortunately, these walls disappeared with the introduction of farm machinery, just as aluminum sheds and plastic sheeting caused the disappearance of the haystacks, those extraordinary blocks of solid vegetation exposed to the winds.

The houses whose walled gardens were most sought after at the time were the Hameau (hamlet), the Petite Maison, the Moutier (monastery), and of course the Vivier (fishpond), which had once been used by the monks for farming carp. The Vivier was occupied by several painters, and by the sculptor Martin Borgord who left his mark on it, then later by John Watson Cox, who worked there on his camouflage effects.

above right

CLAUDE MONET,

The Artist's Garden in Giverny, 1900.

Oil on canvas. Musée d'Orsay, Paris.

above

The garden of Lilla Cabot Perry,

who was a neighbor of Monet's in

Giverny.

The models who posed nude in the walled gardens were not village girls, of course, but the famous high priestesses of the great studios of Paris. They included Jeannot, Gaby, who worked for Frieseke and Ritman, and the very elegant Georgette, who was Dodge's model in Paris. It goes without saying that Georgette's stay in Giverny was arranged following much haggling with the painter's virtuous wife, Fanny.

Nor should one forget those who followed the fashion for night painting, such as Robinson with his Harvest Moon, Will Low, Blair Bruce, Ritman, Breck, and others, who often had to stay until the next full moon in order to complete their work! Paul Morand wrote mockingly: "The sidewalk was slippery so the moon fell."

Rothenstein noted on one occasion that he had painted his first landscape in Giverny. Teatime was a subject favored by Blanche Hoschedé, Frieseke and Edmund Greacen, while Frieseke, Breck, Hale, and especially Butler loved to paint gardens, Watson depicted the masked balls, as did Metcalf and Chambers, Robinson painted the shepherdesses, Breck the shepherds and their flock, Radimsky painted the Holy Pig, and Beckwith and Lilla Cabot Perry preferred portraits. But everyone's paintings featured the willows, haystacks, and the young women out in the sun with their parasols.

top

Monet's stepdaughter Suzanne Hoschedé, photographed by the painter Theodore Robinson. Toulgouat Collection, Giverny.

bottom

The American painter Guy Rose in the fields, accompanied by his wife Ethel, together with Marthe and Lili Butler, and his faithful hunting dog. Photograph, Toulgouat Collection, Giverny.

Many members of the colony were keen photographers and a number of houses boasted darkrooms. Robinson combed Giverny for subjects to photograph and exhausted all the possibilities. His photos provide a precious record of the place and period, since when, of course, many walls and houses have been demolished, roads and paths widened, and new ones laid.

Anna Bergman, Margaret, Lilla Cabot Perry, and Lili Butler played at being reporters, taking seaside snaps, family portraits,

John Leslie Breck,

Garden at Giverny, 1890.

Oil on canvas. Terra Foundation

for the Arts Collection, Chicago.

right

Theodore Earl Butler giving

William Howard Hart a ride in

Butler's mobile studio.

Toulgouat Collection, Giverny.

facing page, top

At teatime, rattan tables and chairs were set up in the garden, along with large parasols to provide shade.

right

FREDERICK CARL FRIESEKE, *Lilies.* Oil on canvas. Terra Foundation for the Arts Collection, Chicago.

above

Theodore Earl Butler giving a painting lesson to his grandson Jean-Marie Toulgouat. Photograph, Toulgouat Collection, Giverny

facing page, bottom

Motorists' lunch at Gaillon, featuring Claude Monet (sitting), Blanche, Alice, Michel and Jean Monet, Jean-Pierre Hoschedé, Jimi Butler and Guy Rose. Every year, the whole family, who loved automobiles, would picnic at the roadside in order to watch racing cars taking part in a famous local race.

pictures of the "naughty Nannie Goat" cart, and an automobile with a flat tire, beside which a disconsolate Peggy Hart is trying to unscrew the wheel while the rest of the passengers look on, wearing the appropriate attire for open-top motoring—furs, goggles, and traveling rugs. There are also photos of picnics and gardens. These enterprising women even made their own postcards and Christmas cards from the photos they had taken.

There were solemn moments when everyone stopped what they were doing and listened to the roll of drums heralding the announcement by the *garde-champêtre* (country policeman) of important decisions taken by the local council. They might concern the amount of alcoholic drink sold, the opening of the hunting season or the closing of grazing land to all the village cattle. Eventually, the speed limit for automobiles became the subject of an announcement.

In the streets of Giverny, the novelties came thick and fast. The "horseless carriage" may be something of a joke nowadays, but people soon became as obsessed with speed as Toad of Toad Hall in Kenneth Grahame's *Wind in the Willows.* Van Vuren, for example, would drive to Paris or to Vernon, or visit the Butlers at Veules-les-Roses, speeding along erratically in a vehicle whose color led it to be nicknamed "the yellow peril." In fact, by 1906 Giverny was the village that had the most automobiles in France! The local council was in turmoil and issued regulations to control the traffic flow. Even in those days!

Even the local priest was affected by the influx. Giverny was not regarded by the local bishopric as a haven of piety, but nor was it irreligious. In those days, priests were often well versed in Latin and Greek and some were competent botanists. When their living was in the country, they traditionally cultivated herbs in their gardens. How fortunate was Monet's arrival, since he brought in his wake so many expert botanists and gardeners such as Mirbeau, Caillebotte, Clemenceau with his sand-garden, and even Guitry, followed later by Metcalf and Butler. Furthermore, it was reassuring to families to be able to appeal to the priest when their recalcitrant sons showed signs of slacking off at high school, and during the summer vacation, all these rascals could be kept busy by a priest offering extra classes. If boating regattas or tennis matches were to be organized, if one wanted to go on bicycle rides or bathe in the Seine, the road to freedom led through a few verses of Horace or Virgil, the discourses of Cicero, Caesar's *Gallic Wars*, a quotation or two from Shakespeare, Cervantes, or Racine. Butler wrote to Philip Hale: "We have Monsieur le Curé here who is giving Latin lessons to Jim. I am so delighted that he is doing it rather than me."

What is striking, when one considers the relationship between the local priest and the American community, some of whose members were fairly happy-go-lucky, is that the newcomers would take care to dress up in their fanciest clothes and attend Sunday mass, even though most of them were Protestants (naturally, there was no Protestant house of worship in Giverny, the nearest Calvinist temple being miles away in Évreux). Butler used to play the harmonium for the services and he even donated a handsome instrument to the parish. Frederick MacMonnies painted a fine portrait of the Abbé Toussaint which now hangs in the church. The priest, a cultured and broad-minded man, contributed to the cosmopolitan ambience of the village.

top

The Vivier pond, formerly the monks' fishpond, photographed by John Watson Cox, who lived there. Photograph, Toulgouat Collection, Giverny.

bottom

THEODORE EARL BUTLER, *Untitled*. Pastel. Toulgouat Collection, Giverny.

above

RICHARD EMIL MILLER,

The Pool. Oil on canvas.

Terra Foundation for the Arts

Collection, Chicago.

right

The Toulgouat family

receive guests at La Dîme,

including Surrealist friends

from high school. Toulgouat

Collection, Giverny.

facing page

CLAUDE MONET,

The Water-Lily Pond, 1899.

Oil on canvas.

Musée d'Orsay, Paris.

above

Claude Monet, Georges Clémenceau, and

Lili Butler on the Japanese bridge, June 1921.

top

Alice Monet and her granddaughter Lili Butler on the Japanese

bridge, May 1910. Photograph, Toulgouat Collection, Giverny.

bottom

The Durand-Ruel family pays a visit: Madame Joseph Durand-

Ruel, Germaine Hoschedé, and Lili Butler. Photograph,

Toulgouat Collection, Giverny.

facing page

In the evening, after a hard day's work, the guests relaxed by playing cards or billiards, and drank liqueurs.

below

The American painter John Leslie Breck. Toulgouat Collection, Giverny.

above right

Theodore Earl Butler, *The Card Players*, 1898. Oil on canvas. Terra Foundation for the Arts Collection, Chicago.

following double page

Family celebration dinner in the home of an American painter. Leg of lamb was served with Yorkshire pudding, contrary to the English tradition, in which it accompanies roast beef. The engraved crystal glasses are from the Paris firm Baccarat.

None of this religious activity prevented the playing of lotto or billiards in the café, the consumption of copious quantities of alcohol or the singing of rousing choruses which echoed far into the night, even in midweek. Even then, some reserve of energy was needed in order to be able to fully enjoy Saturday night's masked balls.

There were houses whose inhabitants shut themselves away to enjoy some peace and quiet, and others which were full of people coming and going—a preoccupied artist, a woman with a sunshade, a maid driven crazy by all the errands she had to run and orders she had to take from people speaking in gibberish, as well as the food she was asked to cook that she hated and did not know how to prepare. Norman cooks did not take too readily to garden peas with mint and sweetbreads with oysters. The Butler household, however, was an exception, as the now weathered Butler recipe book bears witness. But this one household could not, naturally, be expected to provide for the village, and this is where the culinary talents of Madame Baudy at the hotel came into play. Her dining-room became the natural meeting point for members of the colony, eager to sit down to a fine meal after a hard day of activity in the village.

RECEIPES

SCONES

Preparation time: 30 minutes
Cooking time: 20 minutes

Serves 4:
20 g/4 tsp. raisins
200 g/2 scant cups all-purpose flour
10 g/2 tsp. baking powder
50 g/4 Tbs. butter, finely diced
40 g/2½Tbs. confectioner's sugar
100 ml/⅓ cup milk
20 g butter (for the cookie sheet)
3 Tbs. milk sweetened with 1 Tbs. confectioner's sugar
(for glazing the scones)

Soak the raisins in a bowl of boiling water.

Sift the flour and baking powder together into a bowl. Add the diced butter and rub with the fingertips until the mixture has the consistency of breadcrumbs. Add the confectioner's sugar and stir rapidly. Make a well in the center and add the well-drained raisins, and the milk. Work the mixture to obtain an elastic dough. Form into a ball and flour lightly.

Preheat the oven to 210°C/410°F.

Butter a cookie sheet. Roll out the dough with a rolling pin to a thickness of at least 2 cm/¾ inches. Cut out circles 8 cm/3¼ inches in diameter, and brush with the sweetened milk. Arrange the circles on the baking tray and bake for about 20 minutes.

The baked scones should be a deep golden color. Eat hot or warm.

MUFFINS

Preparation time: 30 minutes
Cooking time: 20 minutes

Serves 4:
150 g/⅔ cup all-purpose flour
5 g/1 tsp. baking powder
100 g/⅓ cup butter
80 g/6 Tbs. confectioner's sugar
30 g/2½ Tbs. vanilla sugar
1 large egg
4 Tbs. milk
Walnuts, hazelnuts, candied fruits (optional)
A dozen pleated paper cake cups

Preheat the oven to 180°C/360°F.

Sift the flour and baking powder into a bowl. Work the butter with a fork until creamy. Add the confectioner's sugar and vanilla sugar. Next add the whole egg and the milk. Stir in the flour and baking powder mixture and beat until smooth. If it is too thick, add a little more cold milk.

Divide the dough among the paper cups. Each muffin may be topped with a walnut, hazelnut, or piece of candied fruit, according to taste.

Bake for 20 minutes. Allow to cool on a cake rack before serving.

BACON AND POTATO PIE

Preparation time: 45 minutes
Cooking time: 1½ hours

Serves 6:
400 g onions
200 g unsmoked bacon
800 g floury potatoes
60 g/5 Tbs. butter, cut into pieces
Salt and freshly ground black pepper
1 bay leaf, crumbled

For the pie dough:
200 g/2 scant cups all-purpose flour
100 g/7 Tbs. butter, cut into small pieces
1 egg
1 pinch of salt
20 g/4 tsp. butter for the pan
1 egg yolk to glaze the dough

First make the pie dough (preferably the day before). Sift the flour into a bowl, add the butter, and work them together with the fingertips until the mixture has the consistency of coarse sand. Make a well in the center and add the egg and a pinch of salt. Knead the dough into a ball, adding up to 2 tablespoons cold water if necessary. Wrap the dough in plastic wrap and chill for at least 1 hour.

Peel the onions and slice them into rings 5 mm/⅛ inch thick. Slice the bacon into small strips and cook in a large frying pan until it gives off its grease. Remove the bacon before it colors and cook the onions in the grease for about 10 minutes over low heat.

Peel the potatoes and wipe them with a cloth (do not wash them). Cut them into thin slices as for a gratin dauphinois. Keep them in the cloth.

Generously butter a 22-cm/8-inch diameter cake pan. Divide the ball of dough into two pieces, one twice the size of the other. Roll out the larger portion of dough and use it to line the pan, letting the dough go over the edge all round. Fill the pan with layers of potatoes, onions, bacon strips, and pieces of butter, seasoning each layer with salt and pepper, and sprinkling with a little crumbled bay leaf.

Roll out the remaining piece of dough and, with the help of a plate, cut it into a round the same diameter as the pan. Make a little hole about 1 cm/¼ inch in diameter.

Pour the egg yolk into a glass with 5 tablespoons of cold water and mix well. Brush the edges of the pastry with some of the diluted egg yolk using a pastry brush. Arrange the pastry lid on top and press down well with the fingertips to ensure a firm seal. Brush the pastry lid with the diluted egg yolk.

Bake the pie for 1¼ hours in a preheated 150°C/300°F oven. If the pastry browns too quickly, cover it with a lightly oiled sheet of aluminum foil. Let the pie rest for 5 minutes in the oven with the heat off before removing it. Serve with the heavy cream. To make it easier to unmold the pie, use a deep two-piece pie pan or one with a removable base.

CORN CHOWDER

Preparation time: 20 minutes
Cooking time: 30 minutes

Serves 6:
½ green bell pepper
1 leek
1 large onion
2 garlic cloves
500 g floury potatoes
150 g lean salt pork
50 g/4 Tbs. butter
150 g corn kernels, canned
1 bay leaf
250 ml/1 cup milk
4 sprigs flat-leaved parsley, minced

Remove the ribs and seeds from the bell pepper and chop it finely. Clean the leek, peel the onion and garlic, and chop them all. Peel the potatoes, then wash and dice them. Slice the salt pork into strips.

Melt the butter in a large pot or Dutch oven. Add the leek, bell pepper, onion, and garlic, and sauté them until they start to turn color. Add the salt pork and diced potato, and 750 ml/3 cups boiling water. Season to taste. Add the bay leaf, then cover and simmer for 30 minutes.

Drain the corn kernels thoroughly and add them to the soup. Add the milk. Cook for 5 more minutes.

Sprinkle with freshly minced parsley before serving.

CLAM CHOWDER

Preparation time: 30 minutes
Cooking time: 45 minutes

Serves 6:
1 kg clams (any kind), live
150 g ounces smoked bacon
2 onions
½ green bell pepper
700 g floury potatoes
50 g/4 Tbs. butter
200 ml/1 scant cup milk
Salt and freshly ground pepper
½ bunch parsley

Wash the clams thoroughly and drain them. Put in a cooking pot, cover, and heat until the shells open. When all the shells have opened, drain them. Collect the cooking juices and strain the liquid through a fine sieve. Discard the shells and place the shellfish meat in a bowl.

Dice the smoked bacon finely. Peel and mince the onions. Remove the ribs and the seeds of the bell pepper and slice the flesh thinly. Peel and rinse the potatoes, then cut into small cubes.

Melt 50g/4 tablespoons of the butter and sauté the diced bacon. Add the onions and pepper. Cook gently until soft, then add 1 liter/4 cups boiling water. Add the clam juice and season to taste. Bring to the boil, then add the potatoes. Cook for 40 minutes, then add the clams and milk and cook for a further 5 minutes.

Add the remaining butter and sprinkle with freshly minced parsley before serving. Eat hot.

POACHED SALMON WITH MUSHROOMS

Preparation time: 20 minutes
Cooking time: 35 minutes

Serves 6:

1 bunch small green onions
6 new carrots
250 g/2 cups small button mushrooms
80 g/⅓ cup butter
250 ml/1 cup dry white wine
200 ml/1 scant cup heavy cream
6 salmon steaks
½ lemon, juice squeezed
4 Tbs. chopped fresh herbs (optional)
Salt and freshly ground pepper

Peel the green onions. Leave them whole or cut them into halves or quarters. Peel the carrots and slice finely. Trim off the ends of the mushroom stalks. Rinse and wipe the mushrooms, then slice them.

Heat the butter in a flameproof dish. When it bubbles, add the vegetables, season with salt and pepper, and cook gently for 5 minutes. Add the white wine and cream, and simmer for about 20 minutes.

Place the salmon steaks on a board, slice them in half, and remove the bone. Arrange the pieces of fish in the sauce and poach for 8 minutes. Last of all, add the lemon juice.

Serve hot. Just before serving you could add some chopped fresh herbs (chives, tarragon, parsley).

THEODORE EARL BUTLER,

Untitled. Pastel.

Toulgouat Collection, Giverny.

ROAST LAMB AND YORKSHIRE PUDDING

Preparation time: 45 minutes
Cooking time: 45 minutes

Serves 12:
4 cloves garlic
2 short legs of lamb
4 Tbs. sunflower oil

For Yorkshire pudding:
300 g/2½ cups all-purpose flour
4 eggs
1 pinch of salt
500 ml/2 cups milk

Serves:
350 g mint sauce
200 g/1 scant cup redcurrant jelly

Preheat the oven to 240°C/470°F.

Peel the garlic cloves, cut into 4, and remove the sprouts.

Make a few cuts in the legs of lamb and insert the pieces of garlic. Oil the lamb lightly and arrange it on a large baking tray (or on the broiler pan). Add 200 ml/1 cup of hot water. Put in the oven for 45 minutes.

Prepare the Yorkshire pudding batter 15 minutes before the lamb finishes cooking. Sift the flour into a bowl, break the eggs into the center, add salt, then mix with a metal whisk, adding the milk gradually, while whisking constantly. The batter must be smooth.

When the legs of lamb are cooked, remove them from the oven, and keep them hot.

Collect the cooking liquid yielded by the joints and pour it into a rectangular pan, then pour the batter over it. Bake for 25 minutes.

Cut the Yorkshire pudding into squares and serve on a hot serving platter. Just before serving, warm the mint sauce and pour it into a hot sauceboat.

Serve the redcurrant jelly in a small bowl.

FRENCH-STYLE PEAS

Preparation time: 45 minutes
Cooking time: 45 minutes

Serves 6 :
2 kg/6 cups peas in the pod
1 bunch green onions (scallions)
Large, outer leaves of a lettuce
100 g/⅓ cup butter
200 g finely chopped bacon
1 sprig tarragon
Salt and freshly ground pepper

Shell the peas. Peel and rinse the green onions and slice them into halves or quarters. Wash the lettuce leaves, dry, and mince.

Warm the butter in a deep pot. When it bubbles, brown the diced bacon

gently, add the onions and lettuce, stir, and finally add the peas and tarragon. Season to taste. Add 100 ml/⅓ cup water, cover, and cook gently for 45 minutes. If there is too much juice left after this time, increase the heat and remove the lid so as to allow the excess water to evaporate.

Serve in a warmed vegetable dish as an accompaniment to leg of lamb or other roast meat.

Apple Dumplings

Preparation time: 45 minutes
Cooking time: 20 minutes

Serves 6:
6 small apples
400 g frozen flaky pastry
3 heaped Tbs. apple preserve
60 g/5 Tbs. butter
1 egg yolk, beaten with 3 tsp. water

Peel the apples and core them using an apple-corer.

Roll out the pastry and cut out 6 squares 12 x 12 cm/4½ x 4½ inches.

Place an apple in the center of each square and fill the holes in the apples with apple preserve. Dot each apple with a knob of butter. Bring together the 4 corners of the pastry squares to enclose each apple. Bind the corners with beaten egg yolk.

Cut out small leaf shapes in the pastry to decorate the dumplings. Use a small brush to glaze the surface with egg yolk diluted in a little water. Bake for about 20 minutes. Leave the dumplings in the oven for 10 minutes after it has been turned off.

Can be served with vanilla custard or heavy cream.

Vanilla Custard

Preparation time: 15 minutes
Cooking time: 15 minutes

Serves 4:
1 vanilla bean
50 cl/2 cups milk
6 egg yolks
120 g/1 cup confectioner's sugar

Split the vanilla bean in half and add it to the milk. Bring to the boil, then turn off the heat, cover, and leave to infuse.

Place the egg yolks in a metal bowl, add the confectioner's sugar, and beat with a metal whisk. When the liquid is frothy, add the vanilla-flavored milk.

Half-fill a heavy-based saucepan with water. Bring to the boil, then place the metal bowl over the saucepan and stir the mixture constantly with a wooden spoon or spatula in figures of eight, so that the custard at the bottom is always kept moving. Do not allow the custard to boil.

The custard is cooked when it coats the wooden spoon or spatula. At this point, bring the cooking to an immediate halt by plunging the base of the bowl into cold water. Pour the custard into another bowl and leave to cool.

POACHED PEARS

Preparation time: 20 minutes
Cooking time: 20 minutes

Serves 6:
4 oranges
1 lemon
200 ml/1 scant cup dark corn syrup
1 vanilla bean, split in half lengthwise
1 cinnamon stick
2 star anise pods
6 firm pears
Almond macaroons to serve

Squeeze the oranges and lemon to extract the juice. Pour the juice into a saucepan with the syrup. Add the vanilla pod, cinnamon stick, and the 2 star anise pods. Bring the mixture to the boil gently.

Peel the pears, leaving the stalks in place. Submerge them in the flavored juice. Cover and poach gently for 20 minutes.

Remove from the heat and leave the pears to cool in the juice. Transfer to a glass dish and keep in a cool place until they are to be eaten.

Serve well chilled, with almond macaroons if desired.

CLARET CUP

Preparation time: 15 minutes
No cooking

Serves 6:
1 liter/4 cups dry red wine
1 glass (125 ml/½ cup) curaçao
1 thin slice of cucumber
A few fresh mint leaves
Juice of 1 orange
750 ml/3 cups soda water

Combine the ingredients in the order listed. Add a few raspberries, wild strawberries, or other berry fruits, as desired.

CHERRY BAKE

Preparation time: 20 minutes
Cooking time: 35 minutes

Serves 6:
1 kg cherries
150 g/1⅓ cups confectioner's sugar
2 sachets of vanilla sugar
200 g/2 scant cups all-purpose flour
400 ml/1¾ cups milk
50 g/4 Tbs. butter
3 eggs
2 heaped Tbs. slivered almonds

Rinse the cherries, wipe them and remove the stalks and pits.

Preheat the oven to 180°C/360°F.

Melt the butter in a saucepan and leave it to cool slightly. Use a little of it to grease the baking dish.

In a bowl, beat the eggs with the confectioner's sugar and vanilla sugar. Sift the flour into the bowl, then add the rest of the melted butter and gradually beat in the milk.

When you have beaten the batter until it has the consistency of heavy cream, add the almonds and the cherries. Pour the mixture into the buttered dish and bake for 40 minutes.

Can be eaten warm or cold. For a more elegant presentation, the pudding can be dusted with sifted confectioner's sugar just before serving.

BERRY DESSERT WITH ORANGE FLOWER WATER

Preparation time: 15 minutes
Cooking time: 20 minutes

Serves 6:
500 g/4 cups strawberries
250 g/2 cups raspberries
150 g/⅔ cup redcurrants
4 oranges
6 tablespoons liquid honey
2 Tbs. orange flower water
1 vanilla pod

Rinse the strawberries under cold running water, wipe them dry carefully with kitchen paper, then hull them. Split them in two or in four, depending on their size. Wipe the raspberries with a damp cloth. Rinse the bunches of reducurrants briefly under running water. Wipe them dry and remove the stalks.

Squeeze the oranges to extract the juice. Pour the juice into a deep dessert bowl. Split the vanilla bean in half lengthwise and add it to the juice, then add the honey, orange flower water, and finally all the fruits. Stir to combine, cover with plastic wrap, and chill in the refrigerator for 3 to 4 hours. Remove and discard the vanilla bean before serving. Serve chilled.

Depending on the season, you could add other fruits such as wild strawberries, loganberries, blackberries, mulberries, or chopped fresh apricots or peaches.

LEMON MERINGUE PIE

Preparation time: 30 minutes
Cooking time: 20 minutes

Serves 6:
For the base:
200 g/2 scant cups all-purpose flour
100 g/½ cup butter
1 small egg
1 fresh lemon
90 g/5 Tbs. confectioner's sugar

For the topping:
250 g/1 cup lemon curd (lemon cheese)
2 egg whites

First make the base. Rinse the lemon, wipe it clean, then grate the rind very finely. Pour the sifted flour and 4 tablespoons of confectioner's sugar into a bowl. Cut the butter into very small pieces and add them. Using your fingertips, rub the mixture together gently until it has the consistency of breadcrumbs. Add the grated rind and then the egg. Form the dough into a ball and leave it to stand in a cool place for at least 30 minutes.

Preheat the oven to 210°C/410°F.

Roll the dough into a circle and arrange it in a greased and sugared 24-cm/9-inch pie pan. Prick the base with a fork. Place a circle of nonstick baking paper over the base and cover with small pebbles (or dried beans). Bake blind for about 10 minutes. Remove the pebbles and the paper, and bake the base for a further 10 minutes. Unmold and leave to cool on a baking rack.

Beat the egg whites until they form stiff peaks, adding the rest of the  confectioner's sugar while beating.

Spread the lemon curd over the base and smooth over the surface. Pipe the meringue over it. Brown under the grill for a few seconds.

Peanut Candy

Preparation time: 20 minutes
Cooking time: 10 minutes

Serves 6:
300 g/10 oz/2 cups shelled, skinned unsalted peanuts
200 g/7 oz/ 1 cup lump sugar
60 g/2 oz/4 tbsp butter, cut into pieces

Preheat the broiler.

Arrange the peanuts, well spread out, on the broiler pan and slide it under the broiler. Cook until the peanuts are golden brown, watching them carefully and turning and mixing frequently, so that the color remains uniform. Reserve them and leave them to cool.

Put the lump sugar into a sauté pan. Add 50 ml/4 tbsp boiling water and leave to dissolve, without stirring, over medium heat. Increase the heat and cook just until the syrup starts to color, at which moment add all the peanuts at once with the pieces of butter. Mix very quickly with a wooden spoon and pour on to a prepared sheet of aluminum foil. Leave to cool and harden in the air. Do not refrigerate. Chop the brittle into coarse pieces and serve in a candy dish with after-dinner coffee.

The candy will keep for several days in an airtight metal container.

Pecan Nut Fudge

Preparation time: 5 minutes
Cooking time: 10 minutes

Serves 6:
1 Tbs. sunflower oil
50 g/4 Tbs. shelled pecans
250 g/1 cup sugar lumps
200 ml/1 scant cup light cream
50 g/4 Tbs. unsweetened cocoa powder
100 g/⅓ cup diced butter

Oil a rectangular jellyroll pan.

Roughly chop the shelled pecan nuts.

Place the sugar lumps in a large frying pan, add the light cream, and heat gently to dissolve the sugar. Add the cocoa powder and stir well. Next add the diced butter and boil briskly for about 10 minutes. You can tell whether the cooking is complete by dropping a little of the mixture into very cold water and seeing if it sets. Add the chopped pecans and stir quickly, then pour into the mold and leave to cool at room temperature.

Cube the fudge using a large knife. Serve at coffee time. The fudge will keep for several days in a metal container or tightly sealed jar.

facing page

A window, framed by wisteria,
overlooking the cottage-style,
sloping rear garden at the Hôtel
Baudy. The short flight of steps
that led to the studio is half-
hidden by rosebushes.

CHAPTER IV
THE HÔTEL BAUDY

above and right
Toward the end of the
nineteenth century, pleasure
gardens became the
height of fashion.
following double page
The Hôtel Baudy, with the
museum entrance created in
the former studio built by
Monsieur and Madame
Baudy for their guests.

If the Hôtel Baudy was first cousin to the Hôtel Siron at Barbizon and the Pension Gloanec in Pont-Aven, it was also second cousin to the inn run by Florence Griswold in Old Lyme, Connecticut, at the beginning of the twentieth century. It was a modest country inn typical of rural France at the time. The walls were paneled in polished wood, the marble table tops rested on clumsy cast-iron frames, the rush and cane chairs were shabby, and the room was dominated by a long zinc counter covered in a large number of bottles and carafes over which Monsieur and Madame Baudy presided. A painting by John Leslie Breck evokes the atmosphere of the place perfectly (page 133).

The story of the Baudy is inseparable from that of Madame Baudy herself and her extraordinary enthusiasm for this venture. Her first encounter with the Americans was rather comical: when a bearded giant knocked on the door one day asking for a room, she slammed the door in his face. Following this inauspicious beginning, Madame Baudy was quick to see the possibilities. This unlettered woman, who ran the local village bar and grocery store, had finesse, a generous nature, and a strong spirit of adventure. What makes her particularly interesting is that she seemed to do things because she found them exciting. She had almost certainly never contemplated putting all she owned and more into an expensive hotel project, but she clearly found the enterprise stimulating, both intellectually and emotionally. After all, what other inhabitant of staid Giverny in the 1880s would have been prepared to cook, clean, and care for a

collection of artists who had arrived from the opposite shore of the Atlantic Ocean? She even gave up her own bedroom.

Madame Baudy was a woman with an enterprising spirit and it amused her to introduce some spice into the daily grind of this rather sleepy village. The original bearded giant was probably Willard Metcalf and when he returned from Paris with some fellow students, she was ready to listen. She built a studio in the garden, providing her artist-boarders with a refuge from Paris in the summer, when the heat became stifling and the studios and the academies were closed. The food at the hotel was plain and the rooms spartan, but for five francs a day one could hardly have expected more!

It was especially fortuitous that Metcalf had knocked on the door of the Café-Épicerie Baudy, because in 1885 there were four other cafés in the village, including La Grenouillère opposite the railroad station, where Monet had lodged while waiting to move into his house in 1883. At the time, it was almost impossible to find lodgings in the village. The café was a place to which people came to drink and play cards or dominos. There were also three or four establishments where billiards were played.

A year after her initial contact with the foreigners, Madame Baudy had taken in her first boarders, assigning them to rooms in her own home, as well as other houses in the village. In 1877, she built the studio. This was the first real artists' studio in Giverny, because even Monet's studio, remodeled in 1883, had only one huge vertical glass window which faced the setting sun

above left

Guests at the Hôtel Baudy pose for a photo session
in the garden.

above

Giverny apples and cider were served to croquet players
in the garden of the hotel.

right

Frontage of Madame
Baudy's grocery store, which
she converted into a hotel.
Postcard, Toulgouat
Collection, Giverny.

Giverny — L'HOTEL BAUDY et la route de Vernon
Collection O, Dupont

facing page

Rear façade of the Hôtel

Baudy, overlooking

the garden.

below

Theodore Robinson,

Blossoms at Giverny, 1891-93.

Oil on canvas. Terra

Foundation for the Arts

Collection, Chicago.

above

Flowering roses in the garden of the

Hôtel Baudy.

and not the north, as is customary. In the following year, she opened a new wing at right angles to the house containing additional rooms, and later another story was added containing two studios, one of which would be used by Cézanne. His stay at the Hôtel Baudy is described by Miss Lewis, Mrs. Finn's cousin. Cézanne's visit made a strong impression on her and she gave a vivid account to the Finns, who lived in the village in a house called the Pilotis, not far from the church.

The hotel was opened in 1887. The business cards and headed paper, which were adorned with an attractive engraving, advertised a "Family Guest House. Table d'hôte and à la carte lunches and dinners. Garage for automobiles." Soon, the word "Tennis" was added. The hotel's two courts were built and maintained by Stanton Young, who lived in the refurbished Chennevières mill (known as the "Petit Moulin"). Young organized tournaments which were attended by enthusiastic spectators, including one neighbor who, despite never having held a racket in his life, carefully demonstrated to Young how the latter had missed a ball. To add to the sophistication of her establishment, Madame Baudy asked the Féron horticultural establishment to design the grounds and install an ornamental pool. When the Seine froze over in the winter, she would organize skating competitions. Bruce wrote about them to his mother, telling her how his "Canadian technique" astonished the French. For days when the weather was particularly inclement, a billiards table was installed in one of the rooms of the hotel, proving very popular.

The Hôtel Baudy was full, summer and winter. In the Paris studios, word of the village spread like wildfire. With its endless supply of suitable subject-matter and charming inn with reasonably priced accommodation, Giverny proved irresistible. A headlong rush began, and the Hôtel Baudy became a sort of

CHAPTER IV
THE HÔTEL BAUDY

facing page

LILLA CABOT PERRY,

By the Brook, 1909. Oil on canvas.

Terra Foundation for the Arts

Collection, Chicago.

above

View of the Hôtel Baudy from

the garden.

right

The short flight of steps at the

Hôtel Baudy.

The hotel itself provided plenty
of subject-matter for the painters,
including the scenery, guests
sitting at little tables under the
trees, and people playing croquet
and tennis. Little white parasols
and easels were dotted all over
the place.

American enclave. There were billiards matches with contestants from the village and a masked ball was held every Saturday night. In addition to artists, there were also poets and musicians, who would tinkle away on the piano keys, strum on the banjo, and sing old favorites, with everyone joining in the rousing choruses. Young girls attended dinners in elegant clothes and it became the latest fashion to buy a pair of clogs from Baudy.

Madame Baudy was largely responsible for this success. She created a place that appealed to everyone, from every walk of life, and she made it feel like a home-from-home for all those young people who worked so hard during the day but who often felt deeply homesick during the long evenings. The atmosphere is captured in a photograph showing Meteyard (the painter) and his wife sitting alongside Madame Baudy and clearly trying to communicate with her in broken French while she is doing her best to peel a huge pile of vegetables (page 139).

Many romances began and flourished in the village, not only between American artists, but also with local women. Madame Baudy was party to the love affairs of her boarders, receiving their confidences and passing on their messages. On several occasions, the messenger boy employed by the inn took boxes of violets to Suzanne Hoschedé, Monet's stepdaughter, a gift from the man she eventually married, the American painter Theodore Butler. Butler settled in Giverny and in 1900, after Suzanne's death, he married her sister Marthe. He set the tone for the American colony, living there until his death in 1936.

Eventually, there were so many painters that Madame Baudy became an agent for Lefèvre et Foinet, makers of artist's materials, so she could supply her lodgers with anything they might need. As in all such artists' colonies, some of the "painters" were nothing of the sort. Becktel and his sister, for example, busied themselves for many months in the courtyard of the hotel

above

Painter at his easel in the garden
of the Hôtel Baudy. Photograph.

SPECTATEURS AU G-V-R-Y T-NN-S CL-B.

following double page

After a tennis match, the evening
meal was eaten by the festive light of
Chinese lanterns in the bower.
Honey-glazed ham and broiled
corn on the cob were on the menu.
Cherries from the garden and the local
wine were Giverny's own contribution.

Giverny — Les Tennis et la Vallée (vue de l'Hôtel Baudy)

top

Spectators at the G-V-R-Y T-NN-S CL-B.

Cartoon by THEODORE EARL BUTLER.

Toulgouat Collection, Giverny.

bottom

The tennis courts opposite the Hôtel Baudy were a favorite
rendezvous for the people of Giverny. The ladies took tea there,
so tables, deck chairs, and umbrellas were provided. Locals,
painters, and children also came to watch tennis matches.

Postcard. Private collection, Giverny.

below

KARL ANDERSEN,

Tennis Court at Hôtel Baudy,

Giverny, 1910. Oil on canvas.

Terra Foundation for the Arts

Collection, Chicago.

The rooms were simple but very
well maintained. Hot water for
washing was carried to the hotel
every morning by girls from the
village.

above

THEODORE EARL BUTLER,

Untitled. Pastel studies.

Toulgouat Collection, Giverny.

facing page

The corridor on the second floor
soon became a temporary picture
gallery for the painters who were
lodging at the hotel.

building a boat that never touched the water. The hotel register featured the names of various celebrities, such as Alexander Calder, Bernard Berenson, and Paul Cézanne. Paris was not far away and the little train would unload its contingent of famous people, whom Gaston Baudy would meet and bring to the hotel in his pony and trap. In the fall, the countryside was less populated and thoughts turned to the Thanksgiving dinner which Madame Baudy had learned to cook. Ever resourceful, she had managed to supplement her repertoire of local Norman recipes with specialties from Boston, such as Christmas puddings and Boston baked beans. She even mastered the art of making a good cup of tea, following vehement protests from J. Stirling Dyce, who had arrived fresh from England.

We shall refrain from mentioning the name of the chronicler who told the story of an American dealer who visited Baudy long after the death of Robinson and claimed that Madame Baudy had scraped the paint off the canvases Robinson had left her so she could reuse them as kitchen cloths. This is not an isolated story and such anecdotes are extremely hurtful since no one in the world had more affection and respect for Robinson and his work than Madame Baudy. History will show how carefully she looked after the paintings given to her in recognition of her kindness or those that she had the grace to accept as payment at a time when more materialistic innkeepers would have simply shown a bad payer the door. The difficulties experienced by the artists in selling their work in the United States, as related by Mary Cassatt and Lilla Cabot Perry, would have increased the number of paintings on the market in Giverny and reduced their value accordingly.

following double page

The studio that Monsieur and

Madame Baudy had built for

their guests in 1887.

right

In addition to books, clothing,

and toiletries, painters would

bring their painting materials

in their valises.

For the period June 1887 through 1899, the register of the Hôtel Baudy records some 700 names, although many others have been "lost." It includes all those who, in some way or other, left their mark on the village. Some stayed for a few months only, others for years, and a few settled in the village permanently. They continued to come, people of all generations, over a period of about thirty years in waves that differed markedly from each other. This world, now gone forever, can be conjured up by looking at the paintings and photograph portraits of artists such as Willard Leroy Metcalf, John Leslie Breck, J. Carroll Beckwith, Theodore Robinson, Theodore Butler, R. Chambers, Colins, Congkling, K. Cox, Thomas B. Meteyard, James Finn, Dawson Dawson-Watson, Lilla Cabot Perry, Stirling Dyce, Frederick Frieseke, Philip L. Hale, his sister Susan Day Hale, Ethel Booth, Guy Rose, Edmund W. Greacen, Theodore Wendel, William Howard Hart, Vaclav Radimsky, Mary Fairchild MacMonnies and Frederick William MacMonnies (her first husband), Borgord, Will Hickok Low, Louis Ritman, Theo Van Rysselberghe, not forgetting, of course, the young girl students of Miss Wheeler's school of painting whom she brought over from Providence, Rhode Island.

So much has been written about this phenomenon. There is nothing like fame to inflame imaginations and to create a need to embellish or to bestow a cheap quaintness on the most commonplace events. The world in question has long resembled an infuriating jigsaw puzzle, the pieces of which refuse to fit together. And yet, through the trangled web of comings and goings of these visitors we can capture a sense of what their life was like. The material left to us, personal journals, memoirs, interviews with journalists and art dealers, the recollections of collectors, the day-book in which the price of a paintbrush features alongside a laundry bill and a note about

above

Old wooden paintbox.

facing page

Even the bedrooms sometimes

doubled as studios. To make the

work of her painters easier,

Madame Baudy would order

canvases, frames, and paints from

the famous firm of Foinet in Paris

(now Lefèvre et Foinet).

facing page

An upright honkey-tonk piano and a banjo provided the music for the masked ball on Saturdays. The villagers came to listen to the music, admire the costumes, and dance until late into the night by the light of oil lamps.

right

Head in the studio in the garden of the hotel.

above right

John Leslie Breck,
Mr. Baudy sitting at the café cashdesk at the Hôtel Baudy, 1888. Oil on canvas. Berry Hill Gallery, New York.

bottom

The painter Theodore Robinson in the studio of the Hôtel Baudy.

dinner, with all their omissions, deliberate or otherwise, all plunge us into the everyday concerns and jubilations of the artists and their families. They must be treated with caution, however. For instance, in William Blair Bruce's correspondence, he never once mentions having visited Monet, although he was photographed there and invited to lunch; even if he hated Monet's work, he is here, inside the dusty trunk of history, with a photo to prove it!

There is a mountain of information in these documents, which are mostly personal and private archives, descriptions employing varying degrees of flattery and condescension. From the pile, there emerge articles by Lilla Cabot Perry, Theodore Robinson's diary, *A Chronicle of Friendships* by Will Hickok Low, as well as the exchanges of letters between Theodore Butler, Philip Hale and Peggy Hart or Tom Perry and Guy Rose and his wife Ethel; these documents are redolent with authenticity. Written with spontaneity and an irresistible humor, together they have helped us provide us what is, we hope, a true picture of what it was like to live in this small French village at the turn of the twentieth century.

CHAPTER IV

THE HÔTEL BAUDY

below

Teatime in the courtyard of the
Hôtel Baudy in the early
nineteenth century. Photograph,
Pierre Toulgouat Collection,
Giverny.

following double page

The dining room at the hotel,
whose walls were often covered
with paintings given to the Baudy
family in lieu of payment by
impecunious guests.

above

The traditional Thanksgiving dinner, which Madame Baudy
learned to cook by cleverly combining Norman and Boston recipes:
stuffed turkey, sweet potatoes, and pumpkin pie. Lucien Baudy
commissioned a dinner service (**detail right**) for the hotel, bearing his
initials, L.B., from the porcelain manufactory in Gien.

facing page

Dining room of the Hôtel Baudy.
The checkerboard tiled floor is
typical of the interiors in Giverny.
The walls are still covered with
paintings and palettes from the
period.

RECIPES

GARDEN PEA SOUP WITH CREAM p. 140

GARDEN VEGETABLE SOUP p. 140

CHICKEN LIVER PÂTÉ p. 143

SAUTÉED TROUT WITH BACON p. 143

CHANTERELLE FRICASSEE p. 144

DANDELION OMELET p. 144

ROAST TURKEY STUFFED WITH CHESTNUTS,

APPLES, AND RAISINS p. 147

HAM HOCK HOTPOT WITH KIDNEY BEANS p. 148

DRY CIDER CASSEROLE p. 151

HONEY-ROAST HAM p. 152

PUMPKIN TART p. 155

RICE PUDDING p. 155

BERRY JAM p. 157

ORANGE MARMALADE p. 157

Interior of the Hôtel Baudy. Madame Baudy is on the left,
seated opposite Mrs. Meteyard. The painter Thomas Buford
Meteyard stands between them.

Garden Pea Soup with Cream

Preparation time: 45 minutes
Cooking time: 30 minutes

Serves 4:
1.5 kg fresh garden peas
1 bunch green onions
50 g/4 Tbs. butter
200 ml/1 scant cup heavy cream
1 chicken bouillon cube
Salt and freshly ground black pepper
125 g/1 cup croutons (optional)

Shell the garden peas. Clean the green onions and slice them very thinly.

Heat the butter in a pot and when it is foaming add the onions and peas. Season with salt. Cover the pot and stew gently for about 10 minutes.

Add 500 ml/2 cups hot chicken broth and simmer for 30 minutes.

Purée the mixture in a blender, then return it to the pot and add the cream. Reheat the soup, stirring constantly.

Serve piping hot. Croutons can be added just before serving.

Garden Vegetable Soup

Preparation time: 30 minutes
Cooking time: 30 minutes

Serves 6:
250 g/1 cup snow peas
250 g/1 cup green beans
250 g/3 cups young spinach leaves
2 leeks
500 g new potatoes
80 g/6 Tbs. butter
Salt and freshly ground pepper
1 bunch chives, very finely minced

Top and tail and string the snow peas and green beans. Rinse, drain, and chop into small pieces. Wash the spinach leaves, drain, and chop finely. Clean the leeks, rinse, wipe, then chop finely. Peel the potatoes, rinse, then cube finely.

Warm 50g/4 tablespoons butter. When it is bubbling, cook the leeks gently for 5 minutes until they are soft, then add all the other vegetables. Stir, season to taste, then add 1.5 liters/1¾ pints hot water. Simmer for half an hour.

Just before serving, stir in the rest of the butter and the chives.

CHICKEN LIVER PÂTÉ

Preparation time: 45 minutes
Cooking time: 1½ hours

Serves 8:
4 chicken breasts
250 g boned pork chine
150 g unsmoked bacon
250 g chicken livers
1 large pig's caul (or very thin slices of back pork fat)
2 shallots
1 onion
2 eggs
100 ml/7 Tbs. dry white wine
4 Tbs. olive oil
Salt and freshly ground black pepper
250 ml/1 cup liquid aspic (optional)

Cut each chicken breast into 3 lengthwise. Put the pieces into a shallow dish with the white wine and half of the olive oil. Season to taste, and leave to marinate while the rest of the pâté is prepared.

Mince the pork chine, bacon, and chicken livers. Peel and mince the shallots and onion. Combine the meat, shallots, onion, and eggs. Season and mix carefully with a fork.

Preheat the oven to 180°C/360°F. Rinse and dry the pork caul. Line a terrine with the caul, leaving a large strip over one side, then fill the dish with alternate layers of chicken and filling. Wrap the overlapping caul over the top of the pâté. Pour the remainder of the marinade over the pâté. Place the terrine in a bain-marie, with the water coming two-thirds of the way up the sides, and cook in the oven for 1½ hours.

When the surface of the pâté is well browned, cover it with a sheet of oiled aluminum foil. Leave to cool and refrigerate overnight before eating.

For an attractive presentation, you can pour liquid aspic over the top of the pâté.

SAUTÉED TROUT WITH BACON

Preparation time: 15 minutes
Cooking time: 20 minutes

Serves 4:
4 trout, gutted
80 g/6 Tbs. butter
1 heaped Tbs. ground almonds
12 very thin slices of smoked bacon
2 Tbs. sunflower oil
Salt and freshly ground black pepper

Wipe the inside of each fish with kitchen paper.

Using a fork, mash half the butter with the ground almonds and freshly ground black pepper until you obtain a smooth paste, and spread this inside each of the fish.

Wrap each fish in three slices of smoked bacon and secure with cocktail sticks.

Heat the rest of the butter with the oil in a large skillet and cook the fish for 10 minutes on each side over medium heat.

Serve hot with sautéed potatoes or gratin dauphinois.

CHANTERELLE FRICASSEE

Preparation time: 30 minutes
Cooking time: 15 minutes

Serves 4:
1 kg/6 cups chanterelle mushrooms
Coarse salt
2 cloves garlic
1 large bunch parsley
50 g/4 Tbs. butter
3 Tbs. sunflower oil
Salt and freshly ground pepper

Trim off the ends of the mushroom stalks.

Add a handful of coarse salt to a large pan of water and bring to the boil. When the water is boiling vigorously, put in the chanterelles and cook for 1 minute from when the water starts to boil again. Remove the mushrooms with a slotted spoon and immediately plunge them into a bowl of ice water. Rinse them, dry carefully, and wipe with a clean cloth.

Peel and press the garlic cloves. Wash and dry the parsley, then mince it finely.

In a large frying pan, heat the butter and oil together over high heat. Add the mushrooms, garlic, and parsley, and sauté for about 10 minutes, stirring occasionally.

Season to taste and serve as a garnish for roast meats.

DANDELION OMELET

Preparation time: 15 minutes
Cooking time: 15 minutes

Serves 4:
250 g/2 cups young dandelions (leaves and stalks)
80 g/6 Tbs. butter
8 eggs
1 heaped Tbs. heavy cream
Salt and freshly ground pepper

Wash and drain the dandelions. Warm 40 g/5 tablespoons butter in a saucepan and cook the dandelions for 5 minutes.

Beat the eggs in a bowl with a fork, add the cream and dandelions, and season to taste.

Heat the rest of the butter in a large frying pan, add the egg, and cook over a medium heat. Push the edges of the omelet inward. Increase the heat at the end to brown the omelet slightly.

Serve hot or warm.

ROAST TURKEY STUFFED WITH CHESTNUTS, APPLES, AND RAISINS

Preparation time: 1 hour
Cooking time: 2½ hours

Serves 10:
A 4.5 kg turkey, dressed by the butcher

Dressing:
2 onions
2 cloves garlic
30 g/2 Tbs. butter
50 g/2 Tbs. raisins
2 apples
300 g boned pork chine
150 g salt pork belly
1 bunch of parsley
125 g/½ cup chestnuts, cooked in water
1 egg
3 Tbs. dry breadcrumbs
Salt, ground pepper

Garnish:
400 g/1¾ cups chestnuts cooked in water
800 g small new potatoes
100 g/½ cup butter
10 small apples
600 g Brussels sprouts
150 g lean smoked bacon
4 Tbs. peanut oil
800 g sweet potatoes
Salt, ground pepper

Cranberry sauce:
200 ml/1 scant cup heavy cream
2 heaped tablespoons redcurrant jelly
400 g/1¾ cups raw cranberries
Salt and pepper

First prepare the dressing. Peel the onions and garlic cloves and mince them. Cook them gently in the butter for 5 minutes until soft. Soak the raisins in a bowl of boiling water. Peel and core the apples and cut into small cubes. Grind the pork meat and pork belly. Wash and dry the parsley, then mince it.

Combine all the dressing ingredients—the ground meats, onion, garlic, chestnuts, drained raisins, cubes of apple, parsley, whole egg, and breadcrumbs—in a bowl, using a fork to mash them together. Season to taste.

Fill the turkey with the dressing. Sew up the opening or close it with wooden cocktail sticks.

Preheat the oven to 180°C/360°F.

Place the turkey in a roasting pan, pour 100 ml/½ cup hot water into the pan, and roast for 2½ hours. Baste the turkey regularly with its own juice.

While the turkey is roasting, prepare the garnish. Drain the chestnuts carefully and wipe them. Wash and wipe the small potatoes (do not peel them) and cook them in a sauté pan with 50 g/4 tablespoons butter for about 20 minutes.

Wash and wipe the apples. Cut the top off each one but do not peel them. Arrange the apples around the turkey 45 minutes before it has finished cooking.

Remove withered leaves from the small Brussels sprouts. Blanch them for 5 minutes in boiling, salted water. Dice the bacon and fry in 2 tablespoons of oil. Add the sprouts, cover, and leave to cook for 15 minutes.

Peel the sweet potatoes, wash and wipe them. Put them in a large frying pan with 50 g/4 tablespoons butter and 2 tablespoons of oil. Allow to brown gently for about 20 minutes. Stir from time to time. Season to taste.

When the turkey is cooked, place it on a serving platter and keep it warm.

To deglaze the pan, pour in the cream, redcurrant jelly, and cranberries. Season, stir carefully, and serve in a warm sauceboat.

Arrange the apples around the turkey. Serve the other garnishes in vegetable dishes.

Ham Hock Hotpot with Kidney Beans

Preparation time: 30 minutes
Cooking time: 2½ hours

Serves 6:
2 lightly salted ham hocks
1 small green cabbage
6 carrots
6 turnips
3 large leeks
400 g/1¾ cups unsalted cooked red kidney beans, canned or vacuum-packed
1 large onion
4 garlic cloves
1 bouquet garni
2 cloves
Salt, peppercorns

Peel the onion and pierce it with the 2 cloves.

Put the 2 ham hocks in a pot and add the onion, the whole, unpeeled garlic cloves, the bouquet garni, and the peppercorns, then cover with cold water. Cover with a tight-fitting lid and bring to the boil. Reduce the heat and simmer for 2 hours.

Discard the stem and coarse outer leaves of the cabbage. Cut the cabbage into quarters, rinse, and drain. Clean and slice the leeks. Peel and rinse the carrots, then cut them into 2 to 4 pieces. Add all the vegetables to the ham hocks in the pot and allow to cook, still covered, for another ½ hour.

Drain the kidney beans carefully and add these to the pot last of all, cooking them for 5 to 10 minutes over a low heat.

Serve the hotpot in warmed soup bowls with large slices of toasted whole-wheat bread.

DRY CIDER CASSEROLE

Preparation time: 20 minutes
Cooking time: 3 hours

Serves 6:
4 large onions
2 garlic cloves
2 celery ribs
4 carrots
1 bottle (1 liter/4 cups) dry cider
4 Tbs. peanut oil
1.5 kg beef cheek cut into cubes (or silverside or chuck)
1 piece pork rind (150 g), diced
1 bouquet garni (thyme, bay leaf, chervil, parsley)
Salt and freshly ground black pepper

Peel the onions and slice them thinly. Peel and crush the garlic cloves. Remove the strings from the celery ribs, then wash the ribs and slice them thinly. Peel and wash the carrots, and slice them into thin rings.

Heat the oil in a large pot or Dutch oven. Add the beef and brown it all over, then remove it and leave it to stand.

Put the onions, garlic, celery, carrots, and bouquet garni in the pot. Cover and cook over a low heat for 10 minutes.

Return the beef to the pot, and add the cubed pork rind. Add the cider, and season to taste. Cover the pot and simmer over a gentle heat for 3 hours.

Serve hot with steamed or puréed potatoes.

Honey-Roast Ham

Preparation time: 1 hour
Cooking time: 4 hours

Serves 12:
3 carrots
1 stick of celery
2 leeks
1 large onion
About 20 cloves
5 kg raw ham
1 bouquet garni
2 bottles dry cider
6 Tbs. liquid honey
2 heaped tablespoons Dijon-style mustard
Salt, peppercorns

Garnish:
12 fresh corncobs
250 g/1 cup butter
Sea salt

Peel the carrots and celery. Clean the leeks. Peel the onion and pierce it with 2 cloves.

Place the ham in a deep pot or Dutch oven with the onion, carrots, celery, bouquet garni, salt, and peppercorns. Add the cider and enough water to completely cover the ham. Bring to the boil. When the liquid reaches boiling point, skim off the foam, then cover and leave to cook gently over low heat for 4 hours.

Leave the ham to cool in the flavored broth.

Preheat the oven to 210°C/410°F.

Drain the ham and place it on a large baking tray (or on the oven's broiler pan). Criss-cross all over the ham using a sharp knife. Stick a clove into every place where the crosses meet.

In a bowl, mix together the honey, mustard, and ½ cup of the broth. Use a large pastry brush to paint the surface of the ham with the mixture. Repeat several times while the ham is cooking. Bake in the oven for 30 to 45 minutes, or until the surface is well browned.

Cook the corncobs in salted boiling water for 45 minutes. Drain them, then serve with melted butter and sea salt.

Pumpkin Tart

Preparation time: 30 minutes
Cooking time: 35 minutes

Serves 6:
500 g pumpkin
50 g/4 Tbs. butter
Frozen, pre-rolled flaky pastry dough
80 g candied orange peel
3 eggs
150 g/1⅓ cups confectioner's sugar
1 pinch ground cinnamon
1 pinch ground ginger
1 pinch grated nutmeg
200 ml/1 scant cup light cream

The day before, peel the pumpkin and remove the seeds. Rinse the pumpkin flesh and cut into large cubes. Steam for about 20 minutes, then mash it with a fork. Put the purée into a sieve and leave to drain overnight.

The next day, melt the butter and use a pastry brush to butter a 24-cm/9-inch pie pan. Line the pan with the flaky pastry dough and refrigerate until required.

Preheat the oven to 210°C/410°F. Chop the orange peel into small pieces. In a bowl, mix the eggs with the confectioner's sugar, orange peel, and spices. Add the pumpkin, cream, and melted butter. Mix carefully. Pour the mixture over the pastry and bake for 35 minutes.

Turn off the oven and leave the pie inside for a while before unmolding it onto a cooling rack (this will be easier if you use a pan with a removable base or a springform pan).

Rice Pudding

Preparation time: 15 minutes
Cooking time: 1¼ hours

Serves 4:
100 g/½ cup short-grain rice
120 g/1 cup confectioner's sugar
2 sachets vanilla sugar
1 large pinch ground cinnamon
1 liter milk

Preheat the oven to 150°C/300°F.
Mix together the rice, sifted confectioner's sugar, vanilla, and cinnamon in a glazed clay dish. Bring the milk to a boil, and pour it on to the dry ingredients. Stir, then put straight into the oven. Cook for 1¼ hours. Turn off the heat and leave the pudding to cool in the oven.

BERRY JAM

Preparation time: 1 hour
Cooking time: 30 minutes

to make 6 jars
1 kg/8 cups strawberries
500 g/4 cups raspberries or loganberries
250 g/2 cups blackberries
1.5 kg/7 cups superfine sugar
2 lemons

Rinse the strawberries under cold running water, wipe them dry with kitchen paper, then hull them. Wipe the raspberries and blackberries with a thin damp cloth.

The day before cooking, place all the fruits in a deep dish, sprinkle them with the sugar, mix well, cover the dish and leave overnight.

Pour the sugar-and-fruit mixture into a large, heavy-based saucepan or a preserving pan. Bring to the boil, then simmer for 30 minutes, stirring occasionally with a wooden spoon.

Remove from the heat and use a skimmer to remove the pink foam on top. Add the juice of the 2 lemons, mix well, then spoon the jam into sterilized preserving jars. Allow to cool, then cover, and store the jam pots in a dark, dry place.

ORANGE MARMALADE

Preparation time: 45 minutes
Cooking time: 1½ hours

to make 6 jars
2 kg thin-skinned oranges
1.5 kg/7 cups superfine sugar
2 lemons

Scrub the oranges under warm running water and place them whole in a deep pot, Dutch oven, or casserole. Cover with plenty of cold water. Bring to the boil, then cook for 45 minutes. Leave to cool in the cooking water.

Drain the oranges. Slice off the two ends, then slice them into rounds 1 cm/½ inch thick. Slice each round into 4, discard the seeds.

Pour the sugar into a heavy-based saucepan or preserving pan, and add the juice of the two lemons and 100 ml/⅓ cup hot water. Boil for five minutes, then add the pieces of orange. Stir well with a wooden spoon, and cook at a slow boil on medium heat for 45 minutes. Stir frequently while cooking. The orange skins

should become translucent.

Divide the mixture between six preserving jars, leave to cool, then cover and seal the pots. Store the marmalade in a dark, dry place.

Useful Addresses in Giverny

PERSONALIZE YOUR CHINA:

"Curlicues and arabesques, coats of arms and entwined initials. Personalized dishes are the quintessence of elegance in a tradition perpetuated since the nineteenth century by the Gien potteries."

Faïencerie de Gien

(Gien porcelain manufactory)

Place de la Victoire

45500 Gien

Tel: 02 38 67 00 05

ORDER YOUR ARTISTS' MATERIALS:

Lefèvre & Foinet

10 Rue de Cliscouët

56000 Vannes

Tel: 02 97 46 09 46

Fax: 02 97 46 09 47

Museum of American Art

99 Rue Claude Monet, 27620 Giverny

Tel: 02 32 51 94 65

Fax: 02 32 51 94 67

Internet address: www.maag.org

Open April 1 through October 31,

Tuesday through Sunday, 10:00 a.m.–6:00 p.m.

Claude Monet Foundation

84, Rue Claude Monet, 27620 Giverny

Tel : 02 32 51 28 21

Fax : 02 32 51 54 18

Internet address: www.fondation-monet.com

House and garden open from April 1 through October 31,

daily except Tuesdays, 10:00 a.m.– 6:00 p.m.

Restaurant Baudy

81, Rue Claude Monet, 27620 Giverny

Tel/fax: 02 32 21 10 03

Open from April 1 through October 31,

Tuesday through Sunday (except Sunday evening),

10:00 a.m.–11:00 p.m. Service until 9:00 p.m.

La Réserve Guesthouse

Didier and Marie-Lorraine Brunet

27620 Giverny

Tel/Fax: 02 32 21 99 09

When dialing from outside France, dial the country code "33" and drop the initial "0."

ACKNOWLEDGEMENTS

I am greatly indebted to my husband, brothers, and sisters, and to Catherine Laulhère-Vigneau and Julie Rouart

whose extreme courtesy and infinite patience have been a tremendous support to me.

I would like to thank Claudette Lindsey in particular. I am grateful to Derrick Cartwright, and to Stephen Weill of the Smithsonian.

My gratitude also goes naturally to the Fondation Monet, for family and personal reasons.

Very warm thanks finally to Anne and David Sellin, and to Patrick Bertrand.

Claire Joyes

The editor would like to thank the following for their generosity and hospitality:

Jean-Charles Amoroso and Floriane Lavillonnière at the Auberge Baudy, Christian Jeanney, the Rouart family,

Derrick Cartwright, and Maureen Lefèvre at the Museum of American Art, Giverny.

And for their invaluable help and the quality of the items loaned:

Baccarat, Carmeline, Les Deux Orphelines, Geneviève Lethu, Monsieur Jeoffroy and Janick Schoumacher

from the Gien porcelain manufactory, Le Jacquard Français, Le Puceron Chineur, Marc Campistron,

and Marion Faver.

Heartfelt thanks also to Jean-Marie Toulgouat, Martin Dieterle, and Fanny Stahl.

SELECTED BIBLIOGRAPHY

WORKS IN ENGLISH

Breeskin, Adelyn D. *Mary Cassat, a Catalogue Raisonné of the Graphic Work.* Washington DC: Smithsonian Institution Press, 1979.

Butler, Theodore. Letters to Philip Hale. Archives of American Art. Smithsonian Institution, Washington DC

De Veer, Elizabeth and Richard Boyle. *Sunlight and Shadow: The Life of Willard L. Metcalf.* New York: Abbeville Press, 1987.

Gerdts, William H. *Monet's Giverny: An Impressionist Colony.* New York: Abbeville Press, 1993.

Johnston, Sona (introduction & commentary). *Theodore Robinson 1852–1896.* Baltimore: Baltimore Museum of Art, 1973.

Joyes, Claire. "Giverny's Meeting House: The Hotel Baudy," in David Sellin, *Americans in Brittany and Normandy, 1860–1910.* Phoenix: Phoenix Art Museum, 1982.

Joyes, Claire. *Claude Monet: Life at Giverny.* New York: Vendome Press, 1985.

Joyes, Claire and Jean-Marie Toulgouat. *Monet's Table: The Cooking Journals of Claude Monet.* New York: Simon & Schuster, 1990.

Kilmer, Nicholas. *Thomas Buford Meteyard (1865–1928): paintings and watercolors.* New York: Berry Hill Galleries, 1989.

Low, Will H. *A Chronicle of Friendships, 1873–1900.* New York: Charles Scribner's Sons, 1908.

Low, Will H. "In an Old French Garden," *Scribner's Magazine,* no. 32 (July 1902), 3–19.

Martindale, Meredith. *Lilla Cabot Perry: An American Impressionist.* Washington DC: The National Museum of Women in the Arts, 1990.

Murray, Joan (ed.). *Letters Home, 1859–1906: The Letters of William Blair Bruce.* Moonbeam, Canada: Penumbra, 1982.

Ratcliff, Carter. *John Singer Sargent.* New York: Abbeville Press, 1982.

Robinson, Theodore. Diary, March 1892–March 1896. Frick Art Reference Library, New York.

South, Will. *Guy Rose, American Impressionist.* Oakland, Calif.: The Oakland Museum/San Francisco: The Irvine Museum, 1995.

Weinberg, Hélène Barbara. *The Lure of Paris: Nineteenth-Century American Painters and their French Teachers.* New York: Abbeville Press, 1991.

Wheeler Williams, Blanche E. *Mary C. Wheeler: Leader in Art and Education.* Boston: Marshall Jones Company, 1934.

WORKS IN FRENCH

Aimone, Linda and Carlo Olmo. *Les Expositions universelles: 1851–1900.* Translated by Philippe Olivier. Paris: Belin, 1993.

Hoschedé, Jean-Pierre. *Claude Monet, le mal connu.* Geneva: Pierre Cailler, 1960.

Registre pour inscrire les voyageurs (Guest register), 1887–1889, Hôtel Baudy, Giverny. Original in the Department of Prints, Drawings and Photographs, Phildelphia Museum of Art, Philadelphia. Translated by Carol Lowrey and reproduced in Gerdts, 1993 (see above).

Toulgouat, Pierre. "Peintres américains à Giverny," Rapports: *France–États-Unis,* no. 62 (May 1952), 65–73.

Venturi, Lionello. *Les archives de l'impressionisme.* Paris and New York: Durand-Ruel, 1939.